MARVELOUS WOODEN BOXES
YOU CAN MAKE

Jeff Greef

BETTERWAY BOOKS

Cincinnati, Ohio

Read This Important Safety Notice

To prevent accidents, keep safety in mind while you work. Use the safety guards installed on power equipment; they are for your protection. When working on power equipment, keep fingers away from saw blades, wear safety goggles to prevent injuries from flying wood chips and sawdust, wear headphones to protect your hearing, and consider installing a dust vacuum to reduce the amount of airborne sawdust in your woodshop. Don't wear loose clothing, such as neckties or shirts with loose sleeves, or jewelry, such as rings, necklaces or bracelets, when working on power equipment. The author and editors who compiled this book have tried to make all the contents as accurate and correct as possible. Plans, illustrations, photographs and text have been carefully checked. All instructions, plans and projects should be carefully read, studied and understood before beginning construction. Due to the variability of local conditions, construction materials, skill levels, etc., neither the author nor Betterway Books assumes any responsibility for any accidents, injuries, damages or other losses incurred resulting from the material presented in this book.

Marvelous Wooden Boxes you Can Make. Copyright © 1995 by Jeff Greef. Printed and bound in China. All rights reserved. No part of this book may be reproduced in any form or by any electronic or mechanical means including information storage and retrieval systems without permission in writing from the publisher, except by a reviewer, who may quote brief passages in a review. Published by Betteway Books, an imprint of F&W Publications, Inc., 1507 Dana Avenue, Cincinnati, Ohio 45207. (800) 289-0963. First edition.

This hardcover edition of *Marvelous Wooden Boxes You Can Make* features a "self-jacket" that eliminates the need for a separate dust jacket. It provides sturdy protection for your book while it saves paper, trees and energy.

Other fine Betterway Books are available from your local bookstore or direct from the publisher.

99 98 97 96 95   5 4 3 2 1

Library of Congress Cataloging-in-Publication Data

Greef, Jeff
    Marvelous wooden boxes you can make / Jeff Greef.
       p. cm.
    Includes index.
    ISBN 1-55870-374-8
    1. Woodwork. 2. Wooden boxes. I. Title.
TT200.G73 1995
745.593—dc20   95-11068
                                      CIP

Editor: R. Adam Blake
Production Editor: Donna Poehner
Designer: Brian Roeth
Cover Photography: Pam Monfort

Betterway Books are available at special discounts for sales promotions, premiums and fund-raising use. Special editions or book excerpts can also be created to specification. For details contact:
    Special Sales Manager
    Betterway Books
    1507 Dana Avenue
    Cincinnati, Ohio 45207.

METRIC CONVERSION CHART		
TO CONVERT	**TO**	**MULTIPLY BY**
Inches	Centimeters	2.54
Centimeters	Inches	0.4
Feet	Centimeters	30.5
Centimeters	Feet	0.03
Yards	Meters	0.9
Meters	Yards	1.1
Sq. Inches	Sq. Centimeters	6.45
Sq. Centimeters	Sq. Inches	0.16
Sq. Feet	Sq. Meters	0.09
Sq. Meters	Sq. Feet	10.8
Sq. Yards	Sq. Meters	0.8
Sq. Meters	Sq. Yards	1.2
Pounds	Kilograms	0.45
Kilograms	Pounds	2.2
Ounces	Grams	28.4
Grams	Ounces	0.04

ABOUT THE AUTHOR

Professional woodworker Jeff Greef is also the author of *Make Your Own Jigs & Woodshop Furniture* and *Display Cabinets You Can Customize* from Betterway Books. He has published articles in *Fine Woodworking*, *Workbench*, *Popular Woodworking* and other leading magazines. He lives in Santa Cruz, California.

TABLE OF CONTENTS

This is a book of plans and instructions for hobbyist woodworkers who want to make boxes. My specific intention has been to clearly show with photos and explain with text a wide variety of techniques applied to a range of specific projects. I hope that this "nuts and bolts" approach is useful to woodworkers who haven't been exposed to the techniques before. As well, I hope that more experienced woodworkers can learn a trick or two from what is offered here.

BOX-MAKING TECHNIQUES

Most of the techniques that go into box making have applications elsewhere in woodworking. So box making is an excellent learning ground for woodworking skills that will be useful when you go on to other projects. With that in mind, I included a fair number of projects that involve such skills, like mortise and tenon joinery, veneering, drawer construction, dovetails and the like. And as well, I've also striven to cover in a detailed manner

techniques that only have practical application in box making, such as making turned boxes, band-sawn boxes and small box trays.

MAKING AND USING JIGS

Dovetailing techniques are well covered in this book—from basic hand techniques to several different jig approaches. I provide this emphasis because dovetails are an ideal box joint structurally, as well as being attractive and fun to make.

Do you like elaborate jigs? Try the compound curve router jig I developed for the curved box in chapter thirty-three. If you, like me, enjoy taking abstract geometry and manifesting it in solid wood, you'll enjoy this project.

STEP-BY-STEP INSTRUCTION

With this book I had to choose between presenting numerous designs and presenting quality instructional material on making the designs. This book is heavy on how-to instructional material. As well, I geared the projects for a minimum of repetition, so each project has something about it that is very different from all the other projects in the book.

LUMBER

I have always tried with other books and articles to present projects that use stock wood thicknesses that are available at lumberyards, since few hobbyist woodworkers have planers and thus cannot easily bring their stock to other thicknesses. But in this book, I have not used stock wood thicknesses because boxes are generally small and require thin stock.

MACHINERY

There are various inexpensive planers on the market now, and they work well; or find a cabinet shop that will plane for you at a fee. Chapter one has instructions on doing resaw at the table saw and/or band saw yourself. See chapter thirty-three for a router planing setup that is accurate if slow. Don't let the absence of a planer discourage you; there are workable alternatives that simply take a bit more time.

THE WOODWORKER'S RESPONSIBILITY TO THE ENVIRONMENT

Box building is a great place to make use of highly figured woods, many of which are readily available in hardwood stores. However, I think woodworkers have a responsibility to be conscientious about where they obtain their wood. Some of the most beautiful and striking woods available to us come from regions of the world where, unfortunately, lumber is not harvested in a sustainable manner. This means that the loggers don't use practices that allow the forest to grow back; they take what they want and leave destruction in their wake.

The larger situation with forest harvesting practices is very complicated and goes far beyond the topic of lumber cutting to issues of world economics. Many emerging Third World countries are desperately poor and need the money and jobs that quick lumber harvests provide. Boycotting sales of tropical timbers would cause the wood to lose commercial value, making it worthless to the owners, who might then clear-cut the forest in order to use the land for farming. This effect is, of course, contrary to the intent of the boycott.

So what can you do? Several things. First, when you buy lumber, express your concern (if you have any) to the proprietor and purchase woods that come from sustainable sources. There is an organization called the Woodworker's Alliance for Rainforest Protection (WARP), which will help you find sustainably harvested lumber. Their address is in the back of the book.

Also, look for beautiful woods where you live. I have used a variety of woods native to my region, such as California black walnut, bay, acacia, redwood burl and others. I've also had luck getting interesting woods from local third parties. The teak, mahogany and myrtle I used here came from cabinet shops that were closing their doors and selling off odd stock. I doubt this lumber was sustainably harvested, but at the same time, I know I didn't directly encourage a lumberyard to order more from a nonsustainable source because of what I bought.

And don't forget about commonly available domestic species, like bird's-eye, quilted or curly maple. You can get figured pieces of other common species like cherry, oak and walnut. Many mail-order lumber suppliers that advertise in the woodworking magazines offer such figured stock and will sell small quantities. Veneering is an excellent way to use very beautiful wood without using very much of it.

Wood is a beautiful and plentiful resource that renews itself continually and with careful management will always be available for us to enjoy. Small boxes are an excellent way for us to use this resource in a functional and pleasing way, and a well-made wooden box is a pleasure to create and will always be a valued family heirloom. I hope you enjoy making these projects as much as I enjoyed bringing them to you.

CHAPTER ONE

Cutting Small Parts and Resawing

SAFETY IN THE SHOP

Safety should be foremost in your mind every time you walk into your woodshop. The most important, delicate and irreplaceable tools in your shop are your hands and eyes, and you should always organize your actions with their safety in mind. You can always find a way to make the cuts that you want to without taking serious risk, but this often means taking extra time to make a special jig or fixture that makes it safe. Whether or not you take that time is up to you.

First let's take a look at basic safety. Use glasses, earphones and dust masks to protect your eyes, ears and lungs. Don't wear rings or other jewelry on your fingers, because if rings get caught in a machine, they will pull your hand into it. Don't cut parts shorter than 12″ on table saws, jointers and planers, unless you use a special jig that makes it safe to do so (see photo 2); you can't manually control short parts safely on these machines. Tie back long hair or beards that could get caught in a machine. In short, *think* about what you are doing, and *take action* to prevent the possibility of a dangerous incident.

WORKING WITH SMALL PARTS

Building boxes necessarily means dealing with small parts. Small parts are dangerous to deal with on machines. This is mostly because the smaller the part, the closer your hand must be to the blade or bit when the cut is made. It's also because short parts have less area on the fence or table and can more easily get out of control. There are two basic approaches you can take to making cuts on small parts. The first is to make the part out of a long piece of wood, which is easier than a short part to machine safely, even when it's not very wide. The second is to make a special holder with a toggle clamp that takes the place of your hands as the cut is made on the part, so your hands can be farther away and safe.

If you need a part that is, say, 1″ wide and 3″ long, start with a piece that is over 12″ long, and rip it to width on the table saw using a push stick to keep your fingers far from the blade. Then cut the short part to length from this longer piece, using a special cutoff setup as in photo

PHOTO 1

Use a cutoff box and toggle clamp to cut short parts to length, for 90° or angle cuts. Use a holding stick to steady the part after it is cut off so it won't get caught by the blade and thrown.

PHOTO 2

Make this sliding jig for cutting short parts on the table saw out of any scrap stock. Fit it so it slides along your table saw fence smoothly with no slop. Make it out of material at least ¾″ thick so you can put screws into it for the toggle clamp.

1. You've wasted most of the long part, but that's the price of safety. You could start with a piece that is only 3″ or 4″ long, and make a special jig to rip it to width safely. But I'd only do that if the wood were so precious that I didn't want to waste any of it, because such a jig would be time consuming to make.

Using Jigs

Building special fixtures to make cuts on short parts is an ad hoc sort of thing. Often the fixture you make can't be used for other parts because it's made to work only with the specific dimensions of certain parts and won't work with others. But some setups can be used over and over again. The toggle clamp screwed to my cutoff box as in photo 1 can easily be moved to accommodate different widths of parts. The sliding fixture that fits over the saw fence as in photo 2 can be used over and over, once again by moving the toggle clamp to accommodate different cuts. Things to watch for when using toggle clamps this way are that you don't put the clamp itself in the path of the blade and don't inadvertently raise the blade to where it will hit the clamp.

RESAWING

Resaw means cutting a board along its thickness to yield thinner parts. You can do this on your table saw and/or band saw. On the table saw, place parts on edge and run them through as in photo 3. Make the cuts in stages. First set the blade at 1″ high off the table, and rip both edges. Then raise the blade another inch, and rip again. With this method you will only be able to cut through boards the width of which is twice the height of your table saw blade above the table. This will probably be adequate for most of your needs. If you have a wider board, you can first rip it on the face into two boards of lesser width, resaw both, then edge glue them back together. Note that thin kerf blades are available for table saws and are great for this application because they leave thicker pieces behind.

You may also use a band saw to resaw, and it is capable of taking the entire cut in one pass. Note that smaller band saws have a limited height capacity—an important factor to consider when buying a band saw. Resaw on the band saw is not always easy, particularly when you try to cut very wide boards. Here are a few tips:

Use a wide blade, at least ½″ wide and wider if possible. Wider blades can take more tension and thus deflect less. Use a blade with few teeth per inch because the teeth need a lot of chip clearance during the long cut. Make a resaw fence to guide your part along as it is cut as in photo 4. The fence should be flat and parallel to the blade. Also, the face of the fence must be parallel to the blade horizontally, or the blade will cut toward one or the other face of the part during the cut. Make test cuts in scrap before you cut your parts. Push the parts slowly so you don't cause the blade to deflect—one of the main perils of wide resaw. One way to minimize the risk is to first make cuts on the table saw as discussed above, then complete the cut on the band saw.

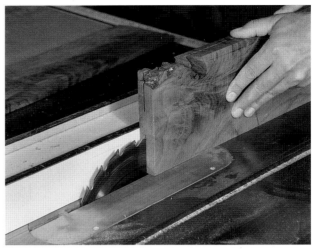

PHOTO 3
Resaw thick boards into thin ones at the table saw by cutting the boards on edge. Always keep your fingers above the blade; don't put your hand on the face next to the spinning blade.

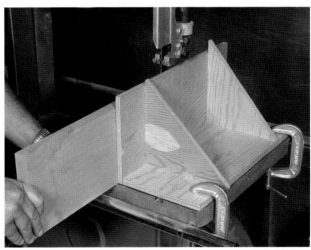

PHOTO 4
Make a resaw fence for the band saw out of any available scraps, such as plywood. The fence must be parallel to the blade, so carefully construct its supports at 90°. You can bring the fence exactly parallel with the blade using the saw's tilting table.

The resawn boards will have rough faces where they were cut. To smooth them, use a planer, or you can belt sand them. Chapter thirty-three contains a router planing jig that does the job accurately if slowly. If you're good with hand planes, here's your opportunity to strut your stuff. The main difficulty using a belt sander or hand plane will be maintaining a consistent thickness, which a planer does automatically. Some cabinet shops have wide-belt abrasive planers, or sanding machines, and such shops usually take sanding jobs from people like you and me. It's expensive, but the result is excellent. Bring in as much stock as you can when you visit, to make efficient use of your time on the machine.

CHAPTER TWO

Finishing Boxes

FINISH AS A TOOL

What's the best finish to use for your boxes? Like the tools in your shop, the answer depends on the job the finish is intended to do, so you should pick the finish that best suits your situation. To help make that decision, this chapter gives a basic breakdown of the different choices each kind of finish gives you.

WHAT FINISHES DO

First, what is the purpose of a finish? Three things: (1) to make the wood surface look nice; (2) to protect the surface from stains, smudges and abrasions; (3) and to slow the rate of wood movement by slowing moisture exchange from air to wood. The first two are obvious, the third perhaps less so but it is certainly just as important. To see why, let's take a quick look at how wood and humidity interact.

WOOD AND MOISTURE

After lumber from the tree is dried, the moisture level in the wood does not remain static, though it does remain far lower than it was in the living tree. As the level of humidity in the air goes up and down, wood absorbs and loses moisture, like a sponge until it reaches equilibrium with the air. As the wood takes on or loses moisture, it expands and contracts, more or less depending on species and the degree of change of humidity.

The problem this poses to all woodworking is that joints eventually loosen after years of moisture change cycles because the wood continually expands and contracts with the seasons. No finish prevents absorption and loss of moisture, but any finish will slow the rate. If you live where there is little change in humidity through the year, this is less important; if you live where the changes are more extreme, the opposite is true.

CHOOSING A FINISH

The three main factors to consider when choosing a finish are (1) the look you want, (2) the ease of application, and (3) the kind of protection you want or need. Those three don't necessarily come in that order. For most hobbyists, ease of application is very important because we

don't have spray booths. Protection is mostly an issue with outdoor woodwork, but interior furniture will last longer if well protected so moisture related movement is minimized. And since boxes get handled a lot, it's best to protect them well so finger smudges can be easily wiped off.

Wipe-On Oil Finishes

These products come in a variety of formulations, which are basically thinned oil-based varnish. Their big plus is ease of application—wipe them on, wipe them off. The look is "natural," which is to say there is a minimum buildup of finish on the wood surface; rather, it soaks into the wood. Thus the wood does not appear to be covered with a film. These finishes provide a minimum but adequate protection against finger smudges and abrasions and may need refinishing in a year or two if handled a lot. Refinishing is easy—just sand lightly with fine grits and apply more coats.

The idea with wipe-on oil finishes is to saturate the wood surface. Apply successive coats until the wood absorbs no more—usually one or two coats is enough.

Oil-Based Varnishes

These traditional finishes are formulations of hardening oils like linseed and tung mixed with resins and metallic driers. Mineral spirits thin the finish to make it flow well when brushed. Varnishes provide a very tough protective finish that resists abrasions and easily wipes clean. Because they brush well, they are a good choice for hobbyists, but because they take overnight to dry, any dust that settles in the meantime becomes part of the finish. Sand with 400-grit between coats to knock off the dust.

There are many different products called "varnish" on the market, with different formulations for different purposes. Polyurethanes are tough plastic finishes, and they look like it too. Use these where abrasion is an issue, like a hope chest that will have youngsters climbing over it. Choose a satin polyurethane finish, as opposed to a high gloss finish, to avoid having your furniture look like it's covered with plastic film. True oil-based varnishes made from tung and/or linseed oil have a better appearance than polyurethanes. Tung oil varnishes are regarded as superior to linseed-based products because tung oil hardens to a stronger, longer-lasting film. But linseed oil makes a good varnish.

Shellac and Lacquer

These finishes differ from oil-based varnishes because they dry solely by losing solvent rather than by hardening of an oil. They dry very quickly, which helps you because you can recoat in an hour or less. Thus dust settling is less a problem. But because they dry quickly, they are harder to apply.

Lacquers were developed for production spray booth situations and are ideal for spraying. Some lacquers can be brushed, but you need to be careful not to brush over an area too soon after the lacquer is first applied. If you brush it when it is half dry, the brush will pull the hardening layer and make a mess. Lacquer provides good protection against spilled alcohol and water and is fairly tough to resist abrasion.

Shellac doesn't resist spilled alcohol and water and is no easier to apply than lacquer. Why use it? Shellac is arguably the most attractive of the film finishes because it goes on so thin and is thus barely visible as a coating at all, while providing more of a polished surface than wipe-on oil finishes. It is also very tough and long lasting, and it protects well against moisture from the air. Brush on thin coats of shellac, as many as six or so. Keep your brush dry, not soaking wet with finish, so you apply the thinnest possible layer and avoid puddles or runs. Use a 1- or 2-pound cut, which means 1 or 2 pounds of shellac is dissolved per gallon of alcohol (the only solvent to use with shellac). Using shellac well takes practice, but the result can be stunning.

Water-Based Finishes

The solvents used for most of the above finishes are nasty to your health, and recently manufacturers have begun experimenting with water-based finishes to address this problem. These finishes haven't been out for long, and many different formulations are offered. When you investigate these, remember to ask the three questions: (1) how hard is it to apply; (2) what kind of protection does it offer; and (3) what does it look like? Many manufacturers of these products claim that they can be brushed on satisfactorily, dry quickly, and provide a tough finish that is water and alcohol resistant. Generally, however, these finishes tend to look plastic, like polyurethanes.

FINISHING SAFETY

If you use a finish with dangerous solvents, wear gloves and open two doors or windows so there is cross ventilation that constantly brings in fresh air. Use a fan if necessary. Don't assume that just because a water-based finish is water-based that therefore it is harmless. Read the label, and protect yourself appropriately from any chemical threat. Don't leave oily rags sitting around; they can spontaneously combust. Used rags should be sealed in a can (a used paint can or cookie tin works great for this) full of water and disposed of normally. This is the only way to ensure that rags will not pose a threat.

SANDING

The purpose of sanding is to level out imperfections on the wood surface and make it smooth enough to finish well. It's not necessary to make the surface of the wood glassy smooth to get a glassy smooth finish. It's the finish itself that needs to be glassy smooth. For it to be so, it must have a base, the wood surface, that is reasonably smooth. How smooth is that? As smooth as 180- or 220-grit will make it is adequate.

Sanding beyond those grits will not improve the appearance of most woods after the finish is applied. The exception here is highly figured wood, such as burl, curly or quilted woods, where the grain is going all over the place. With these woods, sanding to 600-grit will improve the final appearance because it helps the way light and wavy grain interplay. Highly polished wood with very squirrelly grain shimmers like tiger's eye as you move it in relation to the light. This is an effect you want to highlight on your boxes.

When you must sand, sand as little as possible. Begin sanding with the finest grit you can that will remove the defects you need to remove. Sand only as much with a given grit as is needed to remove the defect(s) in question. Then move to the next finer grit, and sand with it only as long as is necessary to remove the scratches left by the previous grit. Then move to the next grit.

Use sanding blocks when using heavier grits (60-120) to ensure that you don't carve a major depression in the surface. Sand by hand with finer grits (220-600) to ensure the paper touches the whole surface and doesn't miss minor depressions. Use wet-and-dry paper with finer grits, and keep the paper wet with water as you sand. This does two things: (1) raises the grain so the paper can cut off the raised fibers and (2) washes away the dust so it doesn't clog the paper.

USING A SCRAPER

Learn to sharpen and use a scraper because a scraper will, in one operation, take wood that is scratched with 60-grit paper and make it as smooth as wood polished with 220-grit.

CHAPTER THREE

Installing Hardware

CUTTING MORTISES FOR HARDWARE

There are two approaches to cutting mortises for hardware: (1) by hand and (2) with a router and template. It takes time to make a template for a router, but once you have it, you can quickly cut mortises sized like the template. When you have a lot of mortises to cut, as with hinges, make a template so you don't end up cutting many duplicate hinge mortises by hand. But if you only have to cut one mortise, as with a lock, do it by hand so you don't have to make a template for only one mortise.

1 LAYING OUT THE MORTISE

Use the lock itself to lay out its mortise. Place the lock upside down on the back of the piece it will fit on as in photo 1. Scribe the outline of the outer plate of the lock with a sharp pencil or razor blade. Also mark the outline of the inside box of the lock.

2 CHISEL OUT THE MORTISE

Use a chisel and hammer to chop on the lines as in photo 2. Chop against the grain first, and always be very careful and gentle when chopping with the grain or you will split the wood. Progressively chop and clear waste until the mortise is close to size, then try to fit the lock and adjust the mortise as necessary. Make the mortise as small and shallow as possible to fit the lock.

INSTALLING LOCKS

To lock the lid of a box, obtain what is called a box lock, as pictured in the photos. These are made to lock any lid or tambour desk top that comes down from above and lands flat on whatever is below. Door locks, to the contrary, lock a swinging door. A box lock has a special keeper plate that attaches to the box lid, above the lock mounted in the box body. The keeper plate has hooked tongues that enter the square holes in the lock body, then the lock grabs these tongues when you turn the key. These locks can be obtained in many shapes and sizes. See the list of suppliers at the end of the book.

PHOTO 1
Use the lock itself to scribe the shape of the mortise to cut for it.

PHOTO 2
Make careful chisel cuts within your scribed lines, and gradually bring the mortise to size. First cut the mortise too small, then r it larger to fit.

1 ALIGN THE LOCK

The keeper plate must be aligned correctly to work at all. First install your hinges, then the lock body with its upper plate flush to the wood surface. Lock the keeper plate in the lock, and lower the lid onto it. The backside of the keeper plate has small pins that make an impression

PHOTO 3

Cut hinge mortises with a template guide and your router. This allows you to make exact duplicates of your desired mortise fast.

PHOTO 4

Make a plywood template for your hinge's mortises with a bearing-guided flush trim bit in your router. Clamp together three pieces of scrap to make a pattern for your template.

in the lid when you apply a small amount of pressure. Raise the lid, remove the keeper plate, place it on the lid matching the pins with their impressions, and use this location to scribe a mortise area to inset the plate.

2 MAKE A TEMPLATE

Make a template for your router and router template guide as shown in photo 3 to cut hinge mortises. The template guide fits the router base and has a protruding ring that surrounds the bit and rubs against the template edges.

The template must be larger than the mortise by the distance between the guide ring and your straight flute bit. A ½" guide ring coupled with a ¼" bit is ⅛" from the bit. With this combination, your template U-channel must be 2¼" long to make a mortise that is 2" long. This accounts for ⅛" at the top and bottom of the mortise.

Locating Screws

A misaligned screw hole can pull your hinge, lock or keeper plate out of its mortise slightly, upsetting proper orientation. Use this procedure to accurately locate screw holes.

STEP ONE Put the hardware in place, and trace around the screw holes with a sharp pencil.

STEP TWO Remove the hardware, and place a sharp nail in the center of the pencil circle.

STEP THREE Gently rap the nail with a hammer, watching to be certain that the nail stays centered in the circle and adjusting it if it wanders.

STEP FOUR Use the nail hole as a pilot to drill your deeper screw hole.

3 PREPARE TEMPLATE STOCK

You can quickly make such a template with the use of a router flush trimming bit. First rip out three pieces of scrap ¾"-thick lumber, at about a foot long. Make the first two at about 2" wide. Make the width of the third exactly the same as the length of the template U-channel you need (which is larger than the mortise it will make, as explained on page 6). Sandwich this piece between the first two to form a U, and clamp them together as shown in photo 4.

4 TRACE THE PATTERN

Put a piece of ¼" plywood template stock on these pieces, and trace the U onto it. Rough cut this area out of the plywood to about ⅛" from the traced line using a band, scroll or handsaw. Nail the template to the three pieces, and use a bearing-guided flush trim bit on your router to make the plywood U match that of the three scrap pieces. The bearing rides on the edges of the scrap pieces while the bit cuts the plywood.

5 CLAMP THE TEMPLATE TO THE BOX

Remove the plywood from the three pieces, and use one of them as a fence screwed or nailed to the template. Where you attach the fence determines where the template rests on the wood during the cut, and thus the location of mortise it cuts. Clamp the template to your box by clamping the fence to the box. Carefully cut out the mortise with your router. Locate screw holes, and attach the hinges.

CHAPTER FOUR

Making Wooden Hinges

WOODS

black walnut

Though more bulky than their metal counterparts, wooden hinges give a box a softer appearance.

HINGES MADE OF WOOD?

Making hinges of wood is not terribly difficult and gives you a wide range of design capabilities. In general, wooden hinges must be larger than their metal counterparts simply because metal is stronger than wood, and thin wooden parts will break fairly easily. But as long as you use denser woods and don't make the area surrounding the hinge pin so thin that the short grain will break, your hinge will hold up fine.

Sizing Hinges

Gauge the size of the hinge to the size of the lid or door it holds. Very small lids can use hinges with wood thicknesses surrounding the hinge pin of 1/8" or perhaps less. But for any lid larger than 8" square, this will be too small. Another important factor is the number of hinges. The hinge shown above is very large and holds the lid of a small box, but it is the only hinge on the box, which

has short sides upon which only one hinge will fit. If this lid were wider such that two hinges could be fitted to it, the hinges could each be smaller since they would be sharing the load.

You don't need to make a separate hinge and then attach it to the box as shown here. You can make the hinge integral with the components of the box, if you wish. However, if you do so, be certain to run the grain direction of the wooden hinge components at 90° to the hinge pin. If the grain direction is parallel to the pin, the wood will be weak in that area and prone to breaking.

1 BORE HOLES FOR THE HINGE PINS

Though your hinge parts will end up fairly short, start with longer pieces and then cut them short later. This will make the procedure much safer as you place the parts on machines. Begin by boring the holes for the hinge pin on the ends of the parts as shown in photo 1. Use a bit that is one third the thickness of the wood. You must be able to obtain wood dowel or metal rod that is the same diameter as the bit to use for the pin. Center the hole along the width of the parts.

To determine the distance that you locate the hole from the end of the part, take one half the part thickness

PHOTO 1

Use a high fence on your drill press to bore the pin holes in both halves of the hinge. Check to be sure that the bit is parallel to the face of the fence.

and add an extra 10 to 20 percent. This extra amount increases the length of the short grain between the hole and the part end, which is one of the weakest parts of the entire joint.

A drill press is the most accurate tool for boring this hole. You can also use a dowel jig. Holes made with dowel jigs tend not to be as well aligned. Use the jig to bore in halfway from both sides, rather than all the way from one side. If your first holes aren't aligned well with each other, cut off the end and try again.

2 MARK OUT THE FINGERS

With the holes bored, mark out the fingers as shown in photo 2. Mark a line parallel to the end and away from it at a distance equal to the thickness of the piece plus 10 to 20 percent. Divide the width of the pieces into an odd number of fingers, evenly spaced, then make Xs in the spaces between the fingers that will be removed.

3 CUT OUT THE HINGE FINGERS

Cut out the spaces between the fingers with a cutoff box on the table saw as shown in photo 3. Raise your blade to the height of the scribed line, and cut the fingers out oversized at first, then trim them slightly until the parts can be forced together with moderate pressure. Leave the joint tight—it will loosen itself quickly with use.

4 SHAPE THE HINGES

Round the edges of the fingers with a stationary sander as in photo 4. You can also do so with a chisel. After using a chisel, you can smooth out the facets left by it with sanding or leave them there for a hand-carved look.

5 INSTALL THE HINGES

Cut the hinge pieces off to the length you desire. For strength, the total length of each side should be at least three times the thickness of the parts. Attach them to your box with glue or screws. Place the hinge, with pin, on the box in place, and scribe around its outside. Disassemble the hinge and pin, and attach both sides to the box base and lid, lining them up to the scribe marks.

You can also attach the hinge with a band clamp. Clamp the box lid and base together in proper position with whatever clamps work best. Place the hinge, with pin in place, on the box in place with glue. Stretch a band clamp around the box and over the hinge to clamp it in place. Remember that with two or more hinges, all the pins must be on the same line.

PHOTO 2
Carefully mark out the location of the fingers, and make Xs in the areas to be cut away.

PHOTO 3
Use a cutoff box to support the piece while you cut away the waste between the fingers. First cut the fingers too large, then make small trimming cuts to bring them to size.

PHOTO 4
Round the corners of the fingers with a stationary sander or with chisels. The radius only needs to be long enough that the fingers clear the other hinge leaf as the hinge moves.

CHAPTER FIVE

Playing Card Box

WOODS

*black walnut
bird's-eye maple
mahogany
alder*

You can make this box with the fancy top panel as shown, or simplify it by using a solid panel of figured wood.

INLAY

This project explores two procedures: (1) stock lamination inlay and (2) the splined miter joint. The stock laminating procedure is explained in the next chapter. You can simplify this project a great deal if you wish by using a single piece of wood for the panel on the top, rather than going through all the steps to make the laminated top. Another variation on this design would be to use hand-cut dovetails to join the sides (see chapter twenty-three). This will take about as much time as the splined miters but give a very different look. If you do this, place one dovetail at each joint in the parts for the top and one or two for the bottom parts.

1 PREPARE THE STOCK

Begin by getting out the pieces for the box sides at the widths shown. You'll separate the top from the bottom after the box is glued up, so for now the two remain together. Don't cut the sides to length as yet either. Get out enough stock for the lengths needed, but keep it in one or two longer pieces for now to make the next step safer.

2 CUT RABBETS FOR THE TOP AND BOTTOM

Cut rabbets into the box side parts for the top and bottom panels on the router table as shown in photo 1. You can also do this step on the table saw, making two separate passes for each rabbet, one pass for each face on both rabbets. Next use a cutoff box with a toggle clamp to cut the sides to length with miters on the ends. Make test cuts to be certain that two miter cuts made on your setup join together at exactly 90°.

3 GLUE THE BOX SIDES TOGETHER

Glue the four box sides together as shown in photos 2 and 3. First lay the parts out flat on a piece of masking tape as shown, then apply glue. Give the glue a chance to absorb a bit into the end grain of the miters, then fold the four parts together with the tape acting as a hinge on each corner. Tape the final corner together.

Check your clamped up box side assembly to be certain that it is square and flat and that all the miters are correctly aligned. Let it dry overnight.

4 CUT ANGLED SPLINED MITER JOINTS

To cut the angled splines on the corners of the box, make a carriage within a cutoff box like that shown in photo 4 (page 13). The carriage holds the box over the blade at about 25°. The resulting slots cut will be at that angle

PHOTO 1
Clamp a fence to your router table to guide the box sides past a straight flute cutter to make rabbets.

PHOTO 2
Start the glue-up procedure for the box sides by taping them together in a row. The tape holds the parts in alignment while you apply the string clamp.

PHOTO 3
Wrap nylon string around the glued sides, then check for square and flatness. Other string (or rubber bands) will work well too. Nylon string has a bit of stretch to it, which applies good clamping pressure.

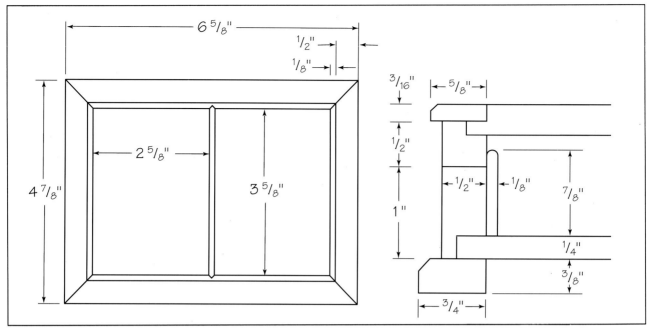

Note that the box sides begin at 1⅝" wide, and then after the top is cut from the bottom, the two together total about 1½". Adjust the depth of the rabbet for the bottom to equal the thickness of the plywood you use.

to the joint edge. Use a stop block clamped onto the jig to carefully locate the slots along the joint edge. Set the stop block so that the top slots will cross the joint edge at ¼" from the top and the bottom slots at ½" from the bottom of the box sides.

5 INSTALL SPLINES IN FIRST CUTS

This setup will only cut slots at one of the two angles needed for the crisscross. Before cutting the second, glue splines into the existing slots, let the glue dry for an hour or so (using yellow aliphatic woodworkers glue), then trim the splines flush to the box sides with a sharp chisel.

6 CUT OPPOSING SPLINES

Now set the jig in your cutoff box at 25° the opposite way, and cut the other slots, again carefully locating them along the length of the joint edge with a stop block. As before, glue in splines and trim them when dry.

You'll notice that the first set of splines gets cut completely through by the second slots, thus those first splines don't contribute at all to the strength of the joint. The second spline and glued miter provide the strength; the first splines are just there for the crisscross effect.

7 MAKE THE BOTTOM

Cut a piece of ¼"-thick plywood to fit in the rabbets of the sides on the bottom. Bore finger holes in this bottom.

CUTTING LIST—PLAYING CARD BOX

QUANTITY	DIMENSIONS (IN INCHES)	PART
2	½ × 1⅝ × 6⅝	box sides
2	½ × 1⅝ × 4⅞	box sides
5	⅛ × ⅞ × 6	internal dividers (trim to fit)
4	3/16 × ⅝ × 8	top border (trim to fit)
4	⅜ × ¾ × 8	base (trim to fit)
1	¼ × 5 × 7	plywood bottom

Top panel made according to instructions in chapter six.

WOODSHOP TIP

Beautiful Defects

This is a good place to make use of small, highly figured pieces of wood you may have around. Often you'll find beautiful areas of rippled grain next to defects on boards, such as knots, or branch crotches. Because they are so close to a defect, you can't use these sections on larger parts for big projects, and you may end up throwing them away as cutoff. Save them for small box sides such as these.

PHOTO 4

Use this setup to cut the angled slots in the box joints for the splines. The two angled fences are at 45° to the table and 90° to each other. The whole assembly is nailed to the cutoff box at 25° to the line of cut. Locate nails and screws away from the path of the blade.

PHOTO 5

Separate the top and bottom of the box sides at the table saw after you have glued in the bottom. Keep your hands on the upper portion of the box during each cut in this operation. Keep your eye on the blade.

WOODSHOP TIP

Cutting Miters on Internal Parts on the Table Saw

An alternate means of cutting the miters on these internal parts is to use your cutoff box on the table saw, along with a toggle clamp. If you use this method, place a fresh cover sheet of plywood or solid wood on the face of the cutoff box as you set up, and position it so the blade will cut into it. This provides support for the small parts as they are cut and reduces the chance of tear-out along the edge of the cut.

These holes make it easy to remove the cards from the box. Center the holes within each half of the box. Use a Forstner bit to cut these holes, if you have one, because it will leave cleanly cut edges around the holes. Glue the bottom into the assembled sides.

8 CUT OFF THE TOP

Cut the top off of the box bottom at the table saw as shown in photo 5. Set the fence 1″ from the blade, and set the blade height just above the thickness of the box sides—no higher. Keep your fingers on the upper portion of the box at all times as you make these cuts, as shown

in the photo. When the top is severed from the bottom, lift the top away from the saw with one hand, and with the other hand, continue to push the bottom through the cut until it is clear of the blade.

9 MAKE INTERNAL DIVIDERS

Rip out thin parts at the table saw for the box's internal dividers. Cut notches in the two longer parts, which hold the central divider as shown in photo 6 (page 14). First mark a center line for the notches, then mark out lines adjacent to the center line to limit the width of the notch. The width should be, of course, equal to the thickness

PHOTO 6
Cut notches for the central divider with a sharp chisel. Apply light pressure so you don't cut through the part.

PHOTO 7
A stationary sander is great for making miters and fitting small parts like these. You can easily take off just a hair more with this setup to fit the parts just right.

WOODSHOP TIP

Safely Cutting Bevels on Small Parts

It's difficult to cut bevels on small parts at the table saw for pieces such as the top border and base on this box. An easier way is to use a sharp block plane. Start with the part as wide as you can, and rip it to width later. Build a special holding jig with thin fences that hold the part on the edge of a piece of ¾"-thick plywood. The fences hold the part in place while you push your block plane along the edge at an angle, gradually creating a bevel.

---

of the central divider.

Use a chisel to make a cut on the center line straight down. Use a mallet to make this cut, but hit it gently or you'll cut right through the part. You only want to go a third of the way through or so. Then use the chisel to make angle cuts as shown to establish the mitered faces of the notch.

10 TRIM PARTS TO FIT

Cutting miters on the edges of small parts like these is easy to do with a stationary sander as in photo 7. Use your sander's miter gauge as shown, or clamp a fence to the sander's table at 45° to the belt face. Fit the internal

parts to the box bottom by carefully trimming the parts to length along the miters.

11 MAKE THE TOP AND BOTTOM

Cut out your top panel from the stack laminated panel described in the next chapter. Cut it to fit within the rabbet on the top frame, and cut a ⅛" lip around the edge of the panel on the table saw or with your router table. Note that the thickness of the lip should equal the depth of the rabbet on the top frame. Miter border pieces for the top and to hold the panel in place. Glue these to the top edge of the top frame as shown in the drawing. Make similar base pieces; glue them to the box bottom.

CHAPTER SIX

Stack Laminating

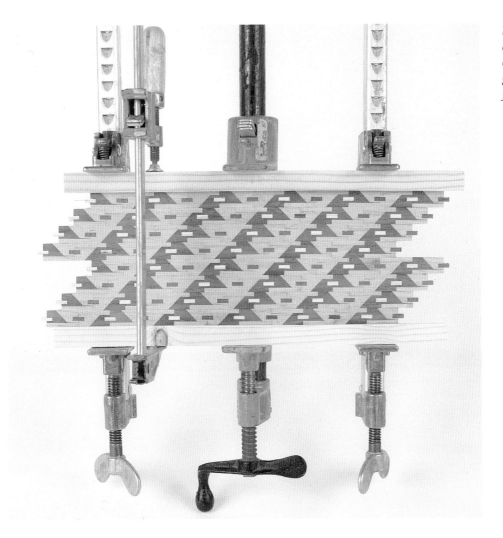

Make a panel with an intricate design such as this or with another design by following a progression of glue-ups and carefully arranged cuts.

"LAYERING" WOOD

By laminating together pieces of wood with contrasting colors and different shapes, you can make striking visual effects, such as the panel shown above. There are many different ways to do this; look ahead in this chapter and chapter seven for two more examples of the same basic idea. *Laminating* simply means layering, and you can layer wood together in innumerable combinations. In this and the next chapter are three ways to do this, but with a little imagination, you can take these basic ideas and come up with other attractive combinations yourself.

MAKING THE PLAYING CARD BOX PANEL

First let's look at making the panel shown above, which is for the playing card box in chapter five. You make this with a progression of glue-ups and carefully made cuts to gradually build the panel in stages. These stages are shown in the drawing, and the procedures are in the photos. The dimensions given here for the parts will yield a panel that is over 1' long and about 5" wide. This is over twice as much panel as you need for the box in chapter five, but it is important for safety's sake at the table saw to deal with a larger panel, then cut it down to size later.

1 PREPARE THE BASE PIECE

To prepare the stock for the first stage, you need to glue together pieces of contrasting colors onto a thin base piece as shown in the drawing. Start with a base piece that is 1/8″ × 4″ × 18″. Make two pieces at 1/2″ × 4″ × 12″ out of woods of contrasting colors, like walnut and maple.

2 CUT LAMINATION PARTS

Make 45° crosscuts on these two parts with a cutoff box and toggle clamp arrangement as shown in photo 1. Make each of the cutoff parts about 1½″ long.

3 GLUE UP ANGLED PARTS

Glue these short angled pieces to the base piece as in photo 2. Clamping to a benchtop edge will keep the glue-up flat. Place wax paper on the benchtop, then the glue-up, then more wax paper, then a backer board on top. Cinch down with as many clamps as you can to apply even pressure all over. You don't need tremendous pressure, but you want even pressure over as much of the surface area as possible. Hand screws are good for this because of their reach, but you can use C-clamps and bar clamps just as well. In this case, you may choose to clamp the glue-up to a thick board rather than a bench edge, so you can get clamps onto it from the other side.

Keeping the parts aligned for such a glue-up is a pain in the neck. You must apply a lot of glue because there is a lot of glue area to be covered. The parts will slip and slide and generally do everything they can to misalign themselves, so you must keep a close eye on their alignment as you clamp down and make necessary adjustments. Begin applying clamps in the center and work your way out, making sure that the angled pieces are both flat on the base piece and that the angled surfaces meet with no gaps.

4 LET DRY, THEN REMOVE EXCESS GLUE

Leave the glue-up in clamps overnight, then take it out and belt sand the top to flatten it. Don't put it in the planer because the short parts could break under the strain and the glue is hard on your planer knives. Use a carbide blade on the table saw to rip off the dried clumps of glue on the edges.

5 CROSSCUT THE GLUE-UP

Stage 2 is to crosscut the glue-up as shown in the drawing. Use the same setup on your table saw cutoff box as you

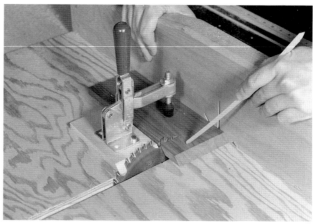

PHOTO 1
Cut off the short, mitered parts with a cutoff box and toggle clamp at the table saw. Keep the small parts away from the blade after the cut by holding them with a small stick.

PHOTO 2
Believe it or not, there's wood under all those clamps. Use a lot of clamps, each applying a little pressure, rather than a few applying a lot of pressure.

PHOTO 3
To safely make cuts on small parts, you need a jig to hold the part for you. Be sure you locate the toggle clamp and its screws above the path of the blade.

did to cut the angles, but cut these off at 90°. Cut halfway through the angled pieces as shown.

6 CUT GROOVES TO REALIGN PARTS

Lay all the parts together on a table as shown in stage 2 of the drawing, and then flip every other one as shown in stage 3. Mark the upper face of each piece with an X. Now set up as in photo 3 to cut a groove in the end of each short part as shown. Center the groove along the thickness of the parts. Always place the face marked X against the face of the jig, so the grooves will always be the same distance from that face.

7 MAKE THE TONGUES

Make tongues to fit the grooves out of woods of contrasting colors. For the sake of strength, the grain of the tongues must run from one piece to the other, not parallel to the joint. To make the tongues, make pieces of the same thickness as the groove and 4″ wide by about 12″ long. Cut off short tongues from the ends of these pieces with a cutoff arrangement as shown in photo 1.

8 GLUE UP THE SHORT PARTS WITH TONGUES

Stage 4 is gluing the short parts together with the splines as shown in the drawing and in photo 4. Place all the faces with an X on one side, and be very careful to ensure that the glue-up stays flat. Let it dry overnight, then take it out of clamps and belt sand both sides to smooth and flatten them.

9 RIP PARTS FOR THE FINISHED LAMINATION

Now rip pieces off the glued-up block as in photo 5 (page 18). Use a push stick as shown, and keep your fingers away from the blade.

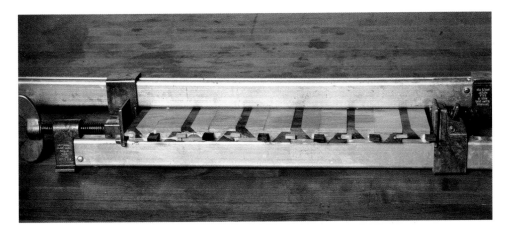

PHOTO 4

Glue the sections together with splines in the grooves. Carefully check the glue-up to be sure it stays flat.

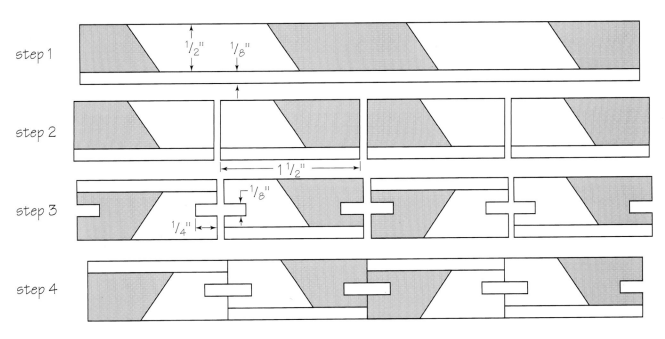

PHOTO 5
Rip sections off the glue-up using a push stick. Glue these sections together to form the panel.

10 EDGE GLUE STRIPS FOR THE FINISHED LAMINATION

The final step is to edge glue together the strips as shown in the color photo at the beginning of the chapter. Note that I offset the strips so that some of the angles line up with each other. Arrange them differently if you choose. To make a different pattern, start by making drawings like the one in this chapter. Begin with a simple glue-up with a few angles, and think of different ways that you can cut it and reorient the pieces to one another.

ANGLED LAMINATIONS IN A BLOCK

Let's take a look at a second technique for laminating together pieces at odd angles. You can use this method as a beginning point for making flat panels as shown in this chapter, or use it to make turning blanks for the lathe. The basic idea is to take a big chunk of wood, cut it at an angle on the band saw, and glue a piece in between along the angle.

1 PLAN YOUR LAMINATION

Begin by deciding just what you want to make, and determine what size of laminated block you want to end up with. Make the piece oversize because after being glued, it will have irregular sides that must be trimmed to make the piece straight and uniform. Start with a base block of thick lumber. I decided to use mine in the lathe for turned boxes, so I found the thickest piece of wood I could find—a 3½"-thick piece of bay about 12" long.

2 MAKE AN ANGLED CUT THROUGH THE BLOCK

Set up on the band saw to cut an angle through the middle of your chosen base block as in photo 6. Screw a fence to your miter gauge, and clamp a stop block to the fence as shown. Use a wide blade on the band saw, at least ½" wide, to minimize the chance that the blade will deflect. Push the piece through as smoothly and straight as possible to produce flat sides on the faces of the cut.

PHOTO 6
Make an angled cut through a thick piece of stock at the band saw with a miter gauge, extension fence and stop block. Don't cut through the extension fence!

3 FLATTEN THE GLUING SIDES

The cut faces will still not be perfectly flat. The flatter they are, the better will be the glue bond between them and the layer between, so flatten them by sanding on a disk or stationary belt sander. If you have neither, use a hand belt sander, or attach 60-grit sandpaper to a flat board with contact cement, and grind the surfaces by hand until they are flat.

4 PREPARE THE CONTRASTING COLORED STOCK

Cut out a piece of wood with contrasting color to fit between the two pieces of the base block. Use your band saw setup to cut angles on the ends of this piece so they will match up with the sides of the base block.

5 GLUE UP THE LAMINATION

Glue the three pieces together as in photo 7. This is a tricky glue-up because the pressure of the clamps tends to force the angled pieces apart. Place clamps on the ends as shown to prevent this. Keep a close eye on the mating surfaces of the three parts to be sure there are no gaps. Doing the glue-up on a benchtop edge helps to keep one surface of the block flat. Place wax paper between the benchtop and the block.

6 LEAVE THE BLOCK TO DRY

Let it dry overnight, then take it out of clamps. The edges of the parts may not be perfectly aligned, but you can smooth and straighten them by taking numerous small cuts on the edges with your table saw.

Now, if you wish, repeat the procedure by cutting the blank yet again on the band saw with your angle setup, but this time cut the angle on a different face as in photo 8. Glue another piece of wood in; this time use a third type of wood for more color contrast.

You can do this as many times as you like, each time adding new angles and woods to the piece. When you are satisfied that you have glued in enough pieces, use your block to make a panel as shown on page 15 by edge gluing rippings, or use it as a turning blank as I did in the next chapter.

PHOTO 7
Despite the use of many clamps, it is still possible to leave large gaps between parts where they ought to be joined. Keep an eye on the parts' alignment as you apply pressure, and adjust as necessary.

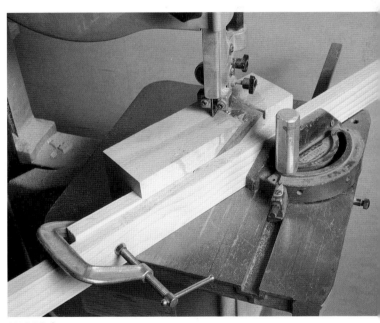

PHOTO 8
Take the glued-up block back to the band saw for another angle cut but this time on a different side so the first internal layer gets cut in two also.

CHAPTER SEVEN

Turned Boxes

WOODS

bay
black walnut
bird's-eye maple
mahogany

Turned boxes have a very unique look and can be made in an infinite number of shapes.

FACEPLATE TURNING

Using your lathe with a special chuck, you can turn small boxes with tight-fitting lids like those shown above. The special chuck is essential to this procedure because there are several steps that require the piece be held at one end only, rather than between two centers, while you work on the other end. There are a variety of such chucks available, and they range in cost from under $100 to several hundred dollars. You can use the simplest of these; all your chuck needs to do is grab onto an external diameter at one end of your blank. See the suppliers list at the back of the book for a source for such tools.

PREPARING TURNING STOCK

You don't need to use stack-laminated turning blanks to make turned boxes, such as with both shown here, but it is certainly an eye-catching alternative. As well, if you have no stock thicker than 1¾″, stack laminating is really your only alternative for getting the thickness you need for your project. One way to do this is to glue two pieces at that thickness face to face, or glue one ¾″-thick piece between them. Choose woods of contrasting colors to highlight the lamination.

Here's another alternative for using both ¾″- and 1¾″-thick stock.

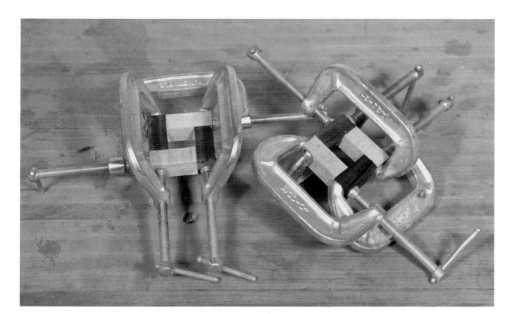

PHOTO 2
To prevent the layers from sliding around when you apply the clamps, apply hand pressure on each layer as you stack them together. Do so for about a minute, until you have forced out excess glue and the two layers begin to grab.

WOODSHOP TIP

Gluing End Grain

End grain will absorb much liquid as the open ends of the pores and cells gradually fill up. Because of this, the joint can become glue starved; the end grain can actually pull most of the glue away from the joint. To avoid this, momentarily dip the end grain in water, and allow that water to absorb before applying glue. Once the glue is on, let it sit for a few minutes before assembling and clamping the joint so the pores and cells can satiate their voracious appetites on a thick layer of wet glue.

1 MAKE LAMINATIONS FOR TURNINGS

Find two woods of contrasting colors, like walnut and maple, and cut out from each wood eight pieces at $\frac{3}{4}'' \times \frac{3}{4}'' \times 1\frac{3}{4}''$. Now glue these together into four small squares, such as the two squares shown in photo 1. Note that this is an end grain glue-up, which requires special attention.

2 LET DRY AND PREPARE LAMINATIONS FOR ANOTHER GLUE-UP

Let these squares dry overnight, then pull the clamps. Before gluing them all together as in photo 2, it is important to flatten the faces so you will get a good bond. This is easy to do with a stationary belt or disk sander. You can also use a portable belt sander, but use care not to round the edges. Another alternative is to glue 60-grit sandpaper to a flat surface, such as a piece of plywood, with contact cement, and rub the squares on this by hand until they are flat. There's no need to use any finer sandpaper after using the 60-grit.

3 REGLUE THE LAMINATIONS

Now glue together the four squares along with two larger squares ($3\frac{1}{2}'' \times 3\frac{1}{2}''$) cut from $1\frac{3}{4}''$ stock, as shown in photo 2. Carefully orient all the parts so they stay roughly centered. This is a challenge because the wet parts will slip around, but you decided to take on woodworking for the sake of challenges, right? Allow the glue-up to dry overnight, and when out of clamps, lop off the corners of the outer squares at the band saw, and the blank is ready for turning.

MAKING TURNED BOXES

1   *ROUGH OUT THE STOCK*

Begin a turned box by roughing out the cylinder between centers. Use your parting tool to reduce the diameter at one end of the cylinder to make a shoulder for your chuck to grip. Different chucks will require different diameters; mine requires about 1½″, which is the widest diameter of the collet teeth, as shown in photo 3. Place the cylinder in the chuck, and tighten it down. Be careful to center the cylinder as closely as you can to the lathe center so it won't wobble as it spins. It's near impossible to get it perfectly centered, but this isn't necessary; just get it close.

2   *ROUGH OUT THE LID*

Now shape the end of the blank to become the bottom of the box lid as in photo 4. Use a gouge to hollow the surface to a depth of about ¼″, then use a skew with a scraping action to make the shoulder of the lid as shown in the photo.

WOODSHOP TIP

Turning Technique

There are two main ways to use turning tools: (1) slicing and (2) scraping. Slicing occurs when you turn the tool edge into the work so it slices off shavings like peeling an apple. Scraping occurs when you hold the tool at about 90° to the face of the turning, causing the tool to scrape rather than slice. Scraping is easier than slicing but produces a rougher result. Slicing is more difficult because if you turn the edge too far into the wood, it will catch and kick back at you like a defensive lineman.

The most important part of making a slicing cut is to always have two points of contact between the tool and the wood. Those two are the bevel and the edge. Rest the bevel of the tool against the spinning work so the cutting edge is away from the wood. Now angle the tool, and turn it so an area of the cutting edge begins to slice wood. During the cut, the bevel should ride behind the cut, following the cutting edge, riding on the surface that has just been cut.

PHOTO 3
The turning blank must fit the collet very snugly. Make the shoulder the proper diameter for your collet or jaws to grip, and tighten the chuck down well. Retighten after a few minutes of use.

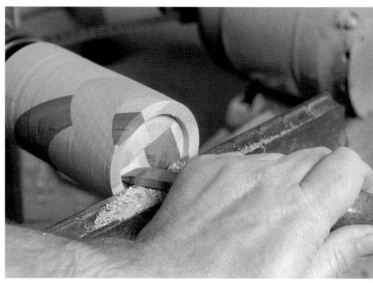

PHOTO 4
Establish the inside shoulder of the lid by scraping with a skew. Cut slowly and gently because there will be a tendency for vibration.

3 MARK THE LID LENGTH

Now determine how high you want the lid to be, and begin parting it from the cylinder as in photo 5. For the sake of stability during this and the next step, engage the tail stock as shown. However, don't part the top away entirely quite yet. Just establish where it will be parted so you know how long the box body will be.

4 ROUGH OUT THE BODY OF THE BOX

Now shape the body of the box to your liking as in photo 6. Remember that you will be hollowing out the middle of the blank, so don't reduce the diameter too far.

5 PART OFF THE TOP

Once you have a shape that suits your fancy, continue the parting cut to sever the top until it is within ½″ of going all the way through. Then remove the tail stock so it is out of the way, and continue the parting cut until the top drops off.

6 FITTING THE BOX TOP

Now make a shoulder on the top of the box body for the lid to fit onto as in photo 7. Use a skew with a scraping cut as shown. Use a pencil to mark the approximate diameter of the shoulder, and then cut close to that line. Once you get close, begin a process of cut and fit using the lid itself as a test to see how close the diameter is. It is important to make the lid fit very tightly because you will do the final shaping of the lid top while it is snugly fitted on the box itself.

If you happen to fit the lid just a bit loosely and it won't stay on, don't fret. Put masking tape on the shoulder of the box to take up the difference so the lid fits very tightly on it. Now set the tool rest at 90° to the center as in photo 8 (page 24), and with the lid firmly in place, shape the top of it to your liking.

7 HOLLOW OUT THE BOX

Finally, remove the lid and begin hollowing out the inside of the box as in photo 9 (page 24). The best tool to use for this operation is a bowl gouge with a small diameter, say ⅜″. These gouges are made for getting into tight spots like this and will allow you to keep the bevel on the wood through most of the cut, which helps make for a more stable, less vibration-prone operation. A larger bevel ground onto the tool helps here too. Still, you will have to scrape a certain amount of the cut, and you must do

PHOTO 5
Use your parting tool to begin separating the lid from the box body, but don't separate the two completely just yet.

PHOTO 6
Shape the box body with a gouge. Try to highlight whatever lamination or grain patterns you have in your turning blank with the shapes you make.

PHOTO 7
After parting the top, make the external shoulder of the box body that fits the internal shoulder of the lid. Use a skew and work carefully, fitting the lid itself in place to get a tight fit.

PHOTO 8
Fit the lid onto the box, and smooth it out while in place. The lid must fit very tightly so it will stay in place during this operation.

so with the tool a good distance from the support of the tool rest, so there will be a certain amount of vibration. When it starts vibrating, stop cutting, and start again gently in a different position.

8 FINISH THE BOX

Once the vessel is hollowed out, remove the tool rest and replace the lid. Sand the turning, starting with rough grits only if there are very rough areas that need smoothing. Work your way up to 300-grit (or finer if you have very figured wood), and apply your finish while the piece is still on the lathe. I use paste wax as the sole finish for these boxes. You can buff it out to a high sheen with a cloth while it's spinning.

Lastly, remove the turning, and cut off the shoulder on the bottom, which held the piece in the chuck. You can grind it off with a stationary sander, or cut it off with a band saw or small handsaw.

PHOTO 9

Remove the lid, and hollow out the body of the box using a small-diameter bowl turning gouge. Work slowly and gently, or you can generate enough vibration to knock the turning loose of the chuck.

CHAPTER EIGHT

Finger Joint Jewelry Box

WOODS
myrtle
acacia

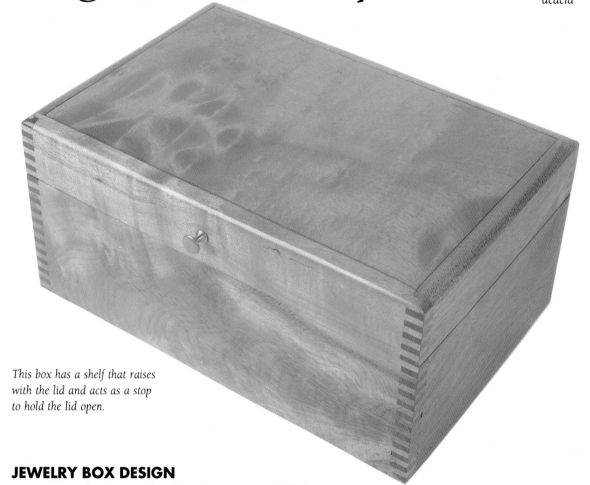

This box has a shelf that raises with the lid and acts as a stop to hold the lid open.

JEWELRY BOX DESIGN

Here's a jewelry box with a bit of a twist, a shelf that rises with the lid. I designed the shelf and lid this way because a removable shelf seemed clumsy since you have to find somewhere to set it down. Also, this design allowed me to locate the shelf so that it functions as a stop to hold the lid open. Making parts with the right geometry so that the shelf and lid work properly is really not that hard. It helps to have a drill press so you can accurately locate the pivot holes that suspend the shelf, but you could align the holes by hand and get a working result.

FINGER JOINTS

Finger joints require careful attention but are not as difficult as you might think and are very attractive when used with woods of contrasting colors. I used myrtle and acacia, but black walnut matched with bird's-eye maple would be a good combination. Highly figured wood is put to best use in small boxes; it makes a visual jewel out of a container for jewels.

MAKING THE BOX

1 PREPARE THE STOCK

The first step on this project, after cutting out all your parts according to the list, is to cut all the finger joints. See the next chapter for an explanation of this procedure. Note that you should begin cutting each joint for the outer sides (other than the shelf) on the edge where the lid and lower box meet. By so doing, the finger joints at the meeting of box and lid will not have any half-fingers.

2 CUT GROOVES FOR THE TOP AND BOTTOM

After the finger joints, cut grooves into the box sides, fronts and rears for the top and bottom. These grooves

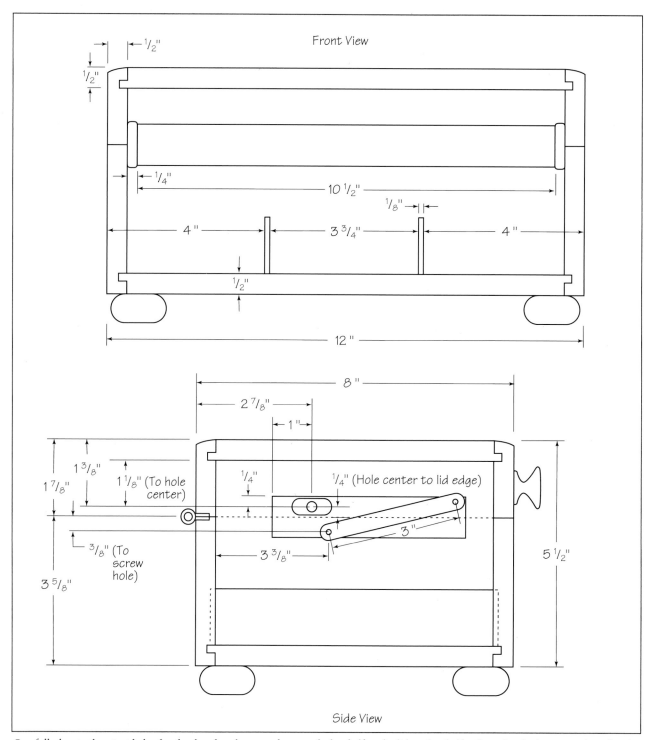

Carefully locate the pivot holes for the dowel and screws that attach the shelf to the lid so the shelf will not bind when opened or closed.

must be stopped at the finger joints or else there will be voids visible in the fingers from the outside. Set up on a router table with a fence and stop blocks located at either end of the fence to locate the ends of the grooves as in photos 1 and 2. Put a ³⁄₁₆″ diameter straight flute bit in the router, and raise it to ⅛″ above the table. Set the fence ½″ from the outside of the bit. With the part butted against one of the stop blocks, slowly drop the part down onto the cutter while holding the part against the fence. Push it along the fence to complete the cut, then lift it away from the cutter. Cut the dadoes for the partitions in the bottom of the box in a similar way. While making these cuts, keep your fingers as far from the bit as you can, and never pass your fingers directly over the bit, even though it is covered by wood.

3 CUT TONGUES INTO THE TOP AND BOTTOM

Once the grooves are done, cut tongues around the perimeter of the top and bottom with two setups at the table saw as in photo 3. First run the parts face down to make the shoulder of the tongue, then run them on edge as in the photo to establish the thickness of the tongue, which should be a slip fit in the groove. Make the top and

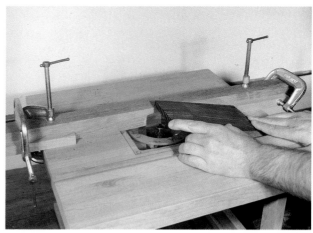

PHOTO 1

To cut grooves in the box sides for the top and bottom, set up on the router table with fence and stops as shown. Lower the part onto the bit, keeping your fingers away from the bit.

PHOTO 2

Push the part along the fence until it hits the opposite stop, then lift the part away from the bit, with your fingers away from the bit.

PHOTO 3

Cut a tongue onto the edge of the box top and bottom at the table saw. The tongue should fit the groove in the sides with a fit that is not very tight but not so loose that it rattles.

CUTTING LIST—FINGER JOINT JEWELRY BOX

QUANTITY	DIMENSIONS (IN INCHES)	PART
2	½ × 3⅝ × 12	lower front and rear
2	½ × 3⅝ × 8	lower sides
2	½ × 1⅞ × 12	lid front and rear
2	½ × 1⅞ × 8	lid sides
2	½ × 7¼ × 11¼	top and bottom
2	⅛ × 1⅜ × 7¼	lower dividers
2	½ × ⅞ × 10½	shelf front and rear
2	½ × ⅞ × 5½	shelf sides
1	⅛ × 5½ × 10½	shelf bottom
4	⅛ × ⅞ × 4¾	shelf dividers
2	⅛ × ⅞ × 7⅝	shelf dividers
1	½ × 2 × 4½	ring insert
2	¼ × ½ × 1	shelf hinge spacers
2	¼ × ⅜ × 3½	levers

Any chosen configuration feet ⅛″, ¼″ dowels

bottom ¹⁄₁₆″ less in width than the space in which they will fit so they can expand a bit with moisture variations and not be constricted by the frames in which they are held.

4 LOCATE THE PIVOT POINTS FOR THE SHELF

It is important that the pivot points for the shelf and its levers be carefully located on both sides, otherwise the shelf could bind as it is closed. Locate these holes on a drill press if possible. Bore the ¼″ holes in the lid sides and shelf sides as in photo 4. Use a similar setup to bore the holes for the lever screws in the lower box sides. Pretest a screw in a hole drilled by the bit you use here to be sure it is the right size, but don't drill the lever screw holes in the shelf sides yet; this will be done after the box is assembled to assure a location that will not cause binding.

Note that the ¼″ holes locate the shelf such that when the lid is opened to a full vertical position, the shelf contacts the inside of the lid top and holds it open. The distance from the ¼″ dowel center to the inside of the box top must be ⅛″ greater than the distance between this center and the top rear of the shelf. Since the dowel center is at the top of the shelf side, the shelf bottom rear is far enough away from the dowel that it will contact the top.

Bore holes in the levers for screws as in photo 5, and countersink the holes so the screwheads will be recessed behind the face of the lever. Note that you need countersinks on opposite faces of the levers since the screws go in opposite directions. Make the distance between the hole centers 3″.

5 MAKE SHELF DIVIDERS

Make the dividers in the shelf from stock the same thickness as the blade kerf that you use to cut their slots. Plane the stock to match, or rip it out at the table saw. Use the setup shown in photo 6 to safely cut the slots. Use a toggle clamp to hold short parts, not your fingers. Clamp a stop block to the fence as shown to establish the distance of each slot from the part end. The parts fit together as in photo 7. If you wish, cut shallow dadoes on the inside of the shelf sides for the dividers to fit in; or eliminate these, and cut the dividers just long enough to fit inside the shelf with no dadoes.

6 MAKE THE RING HOLDER

For the ring holder on the left side of the shelf, start with a piece ½″ × 4½″ × 12″, and cut the ring slots along the

PHOTO 4

Set up at the drill press with a fence and stop block as shown to locate the holes in the shelf and box sides that will hold the shelf to the lid and levers.

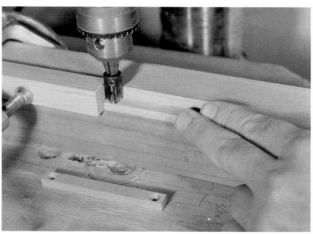

PHOTO 5

Use a similar setup at the drill press for the levers. Countersink these holes so the screwheads will be recessed behind the face of the levers.

PHOTO 6

Safely cut slots in small parts, such as the shelf dividers, by holding them to a jig with a toggle clamp as they are cut.

grain on the table saw with the blade raised to ⅜". Then cut a piece 1⅞" long from this piece. If you are making only one box, this is very wasteful, but it is far safer than trying to cut slots into a piece that starts so small.

7 GLUE UP THE BOX

Glue up the parts, checking to be sure that both lid and lower box are square. Don't glue in the top and bottom, and take pains to see to it that glue doesn't squeeze from the finger joints into the dadoes for these. Once again, this is to avoid restricting moisture-related movement.

8 INSTALL PINS IN THE FINGER JOINTS

After the glue is set, bore ⅛" holes ½" deep at the top and bottom of the finger joints. Glue and insert ⅛" dowels. These pins are just for looks; the glue is more than enough to hold the joints together. Then you are ready for sanding and installing the lid hinges.

9 MAKE THE FEET

I turned the box feet on the lathe as in photo 8, then cut each one out on the band saw. Square feet of any design would make a good substitute if you haven't access to a lathe. Mine were screwed to the bottom from inside the lower box; this should be done before the shelf is installed.

10 MAKE THE BOTTOM PLATE

Make the bottom plate on the shelf from a piece of solid stock ⅛" × 5½" × 10½", and secure it with roundheaded screws and washers. Bore the holes in the plate far larger than the shank of the screws, and use washers large enough to cover the holes. Again, this is to accommodate moisture-related movement.

11 INSTALL THE LEVERS

Make and glue the two small spacers onto the shelf sides, lining up the holes. Install the levers onto the lower box with screws into the predrilled holes, and then install the shelf into the lid by inserting the dowels through the shelf holes into the lid holes. Next drill one of the lever holes into one side of the shelf at 3½" from the dowel hole center and midway vertically on the shelf. Install this screw. To locate the other shelf lever screw hole, hold the lid just open so you can see the shelf side, and hold the unattached lever up to the shelf with a small

PHOTO 7
Fit the internal dividers together with overlapping slots as shown.

PHOTO 8
I'm not very good with a skew on the lathe, so I do turning the safe way by using the tool to scrape rather than cut. The difference is that when scraping, the tool edge is at about 90° to the work, rather than turned into it to take a slice. Slicing produces a smoother cut, but it's hard to control and can kick back at you. Always wear a face mask when turning.

nail through the screw hole. Scribe a small arc along the midsection of the shelf with the nail. Open the lid, and measure up from the bottom of the shelf onto the arc the same height as the hole on the other side. Bore here for the lever screw hole, install the screw, and you're ready for a touch-up sanding and the finish.

CHAPTER NINE

Making Finger Joints

THE FINGER JOINT JIG

With this jig you can make finger joints on a table saw or a router table. You need to have some means of pushing the jig across the blade or bit, such as a miter gauge or a cutoff box. Use a ripping blade when setting up on the table saw because it leaves a square end on the cut. Crosscut and combination blades will leave a small *V*, which is slightly visible on the finished joint. A dado can be used for a wider finger; in this case, adjust the tongue thickness and distance from the blade accordingly. On a router table, the width of your fingers will be determined by the diameter of the straight flute bit you use for the cuts between fingers.

The jig has a small tongue alongside the path of the blade set to allow progressive cuts in the part, each cut being referred to the last by placing the last cut over the tongue as in photos 1 and 2.

MAKING THE JIG

1 MAKE THE TONGUE

Begin making the jig by making this tongue. Make the thickness of the tongue the same dimension as the saw kerf so each cut will fit on the tongue with no looseness. Any looseness will cause a variation in spacing between cuts, causing a poorly fitting or nonfitting joint.

2 PREPARE THE JIG STOCK

Make the jig from two pieces of stock approximately 3/4" × 4" × 20". Screw the first to your miter fence, and clamp the second to the first. The second has the tongue and is clamped onto its mate so it can be adjusted back and forth to align carefully the distance between the tongue and blade. This is the critical adjustment that determines the fit of the joints.

3 ADJUST THE JIG

When first setting up the jig, set the distance between the tongue and the blade by measuring with a rule, and

PHOTO 1
The jig consists of two long boards and a small tongue. One board is attached to a miter gauge, the other is clamped to the first. The tongue is fitted into a slot in the clamped board.

set the distance equal to the thickness of the cut made by the blade. Make small adjustments by loosening the C-clamps on the jig and gently rapping with a hammer, moving it just a hair. After making such an adjustment, retighten the clamps. Once you have a blade and tongue setup adjusted as close as possible by measure, make the final adjustment of the distance from the tongue to the blade by making test joints on scrap.

CUTTING FINGER JOINTS

1 MAKING TEST CUTS

To make one side of a joint, first place the piece vertically in the jig butted up against the tongue, and make a cut. Pull the jig back across the blade, lift the piece over the tongue, and slide the first cut onto the tongue. Again push, retract, and laterally advance the piece, and continue the process until you have gone the width of the part as in photo 2.

PHOTO 2

Use the tongue as the reference point for making each of the cuts in the joints. After each cut, lift the part off the tongue and place the last cut over the tongue. Now you're set up for the next cut.

PHOTO 3

On matching parts, you need to make a cut on the very edge of the part for the first cut. Do so with a spacer placed between the tongue and part as shown.

2 CUTTING THE MATING PIECE

Note that the joint starts with a tongue at the point where you began, thus the mating piece must have a cut in this place in order for the edges of the parts to line up. To achieve this, insert a spacer between the tongue and blade for the first cut on the mating piece as in photo 3. Make the spacer equal in thickness to the distance from the blade to the tongue. Since the spacer and tongue are both the same thickness, make them both when you make the tongue.

3 TEST FIT THE SIDES AND MAKE ADJUSTMENTS

When you have your first two test pieces, you will quickly see whether the tongue-to-blade distance is correct by the fit of the two parts. When the distance is too great,

the fingers are too fat to fit the grooves; when too little, they are loose. Scribe a line across the tops of the two main jig pieces, then adjust the distance from tongue to blade watching this scribe to see how much you have moved the clamped jig piece. A little goes a long way.

ACCURATELY AND SAFELY CUTTING FINGER JOINTS

When you are running your pieces through the progressive cuts for each joint, be careful to always hold each part with the same pressure from your hands and with your hands in the same position. This is because even if the tongue has a tight fit in the cut, you can vary the position of the cut slightly by pushing one way or the other. If you happen to push one way on all the cuts for one piece and then push the other way for all the cuts on the mating piece, the combined difference can offset the fingers enough to prevent them from fitting as in photo 4. But with a tight fit at the tongue and consistent holding, the result will be quite uniform and well fitting. Tear-out can be a problem with brittle or highly figured woods. Placing a cover sheet behind the piece will help.

Keep Your Eye on the Blade

While making cuts, always watch the blade as you push the wood into it. This is the best safeguard to prevent yourself from pushing your fingers into the blade. Don't look off to the side while you push the jig across the blade.

Cutting Long Joints

When you make joints that have more than eight or ten tongues, it's best to check the fit of the joints while you are in the process of cutting them. You may find that halfway through cutting the mating piece, the fit is a bit loose or tight. To make the parts match, apply pressure one way or the other during the next five or six cuts while the part is loaded in the jig.

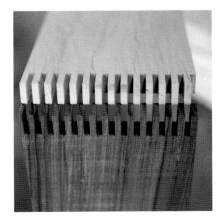

PHOTO 4

This misaligned joint was caused by pushing the lighter colored board to one side during all of its cuts. The combined effect is to offset the spacing enough that the joint doesn't fit.

CHAPTER TEN

Box of Drawers

WOODS
quartersawn red oak

Matched grain on numerous drawer fronts gives a box a very distinctive look. You'll need to start with a wide piece of figured lumber, such as this quartersawn oak.

GRAIN MATCHING

I built this small box as a tool chest not too long ago and decided that the design could function just as well for holding jewelry or anything else. Grain matching the drawer fronts on a box of drawers like this gives it a special appeal. I took all the drawer fronts from a single piece of quartersawn oak with wonderful figure. Making those drawers is covered in the next chapter. Here let's focus on building the carcass that holds them.

1 PREPARE THE STOCK

Get out the parts for the four outer box sides and internal dividers. Join the four corners of the outer sides with finger joints as explained in chapter nine, or if you like, use another joint such as dovetails or one of the joints shown in the next chapter. Note, however, that you can't use an interlocking joint that must slide together like the

joint used to make the drawers. The reason is that you can't slide these joints together on a box like this *and* fit the tenons for the internal dividers at the same time.

If you use finger joints as shown, be extra cautious as you cut the joints. Wide finger joints like this can easily become misaligned while they are cut if you accidentally push too much one way or the other. Check the joints halfway through cutting them, and if necessary, adjust how you hold them in place in the jig to alter the fit.

2 MARK THE SIDES FOR THROUGH MORTISES

Mark the outer box sides and internal dividers for the mortises that join the dividers to themselves and the sides. Take extra care as you mark these out so the mortises will be accurately located. The drawers will not fit properly if the spaces for them are too small.

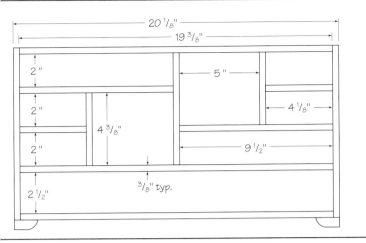

Carefully align the carcass sides and internal parts so the spaces for the drawers are square and uniform.

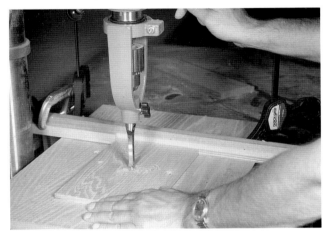

PHOTO 1

A drill press chisel mortiser is a good way to cut a lot of mortises in little time. Most drill press manufacturers offer this attachment for their tools.

3 CUT THE MORTISES

Set up on the drill press with a mortising attachment to cut three mortises along each joint as in photo 1. (See chapter twenty-seven for more information on mortising techniques.) Place a fence on the drill press to locate the distance of the mortises from the end of the part. Use a stop block on the fence as shown to locate the distance from the edge of the part for the mortises. You will have many duplicate setups between similar parts, so take advantage of this fact and cut as many like-located holes on each setup as you can.

Locate mortises at ½" from the edges of parts and at the center. Note that the internal parts are not as wide as the outer parts. This is to make way for the plywood back that fits within the outer sides and against the back of the internal parts.

CUTTING LIST—BOX OF DRAWERS

All stock is ⅜″ thick except drawer bottoms and back, which are ¼″ ply. Drawer sides and backs can be of any wood.

QUANTITY	DIMENSIONS (IN INCHES)	PART
2	7 × 20⅛	top and bottom
2	7 × 10⅜	sides
1	6¾ × 20⅛	shelf
2	6¾ × 10¼	shelves
1	6¾ × 7½	vertical dividers
2	6¾ × 5⅛	vertical dividers
2	6¾ × 4⅞	shelves
1	2½ × 19⅜	drawer faces
2	2 × 9½	drawer faces
4	2 × 4⅛	drawer faces
2	4⅜ × 5	drawer faces
1	2½ × 19⅜	drawer sides and backs
2	2 × 9½	drawer sides and backs
4	2 × 4⅛	drawer sides and backs
2	4⅜ × 5	drawer sides and backs
2	2½ × 6⅜	drawer sides and backs
12	2 × 6⅜	drawer sides and backs
4	4⅜ × 6⅜	drawer sides and backs
1	18⅞ × 5⅞	drawer bottoms
2	9 × 5⅞	drawer bottoms
2	4½ × 5⅞	drawer bottoms
4	3⅝ × 5⅞	drawer bottoms
1	¼ × 9⅝ × 19⅜	back

4 MARK THE TENON SIDES

Use the mortises you have cut to mark out the sides of the tenons you will cut on the ends of the internal parts as in photo 2. Carefully mark each part so you know which side is toward the front of the box and which face is up, as well as whether the part is located on the right or left of the box.

5 CUT THE TENONS

Screw a 4"-tall fence to your miter gauge as in photo 3. Set up a ½"-wide dado in the saw, and raise it to ⅜". Place the internal parts on end on the miter gauge fence as shown, and cut away the waste between tenons, carefully noting the marked location of each tenon. Test fit each part end to its corresponding mortises, and make adjustments in the tenon widths until they fit.

6 GLUE UP THE BOX

Fit all the internal parts together, and fit them to the external sides as shown in photo 4. You don't need to glue the mortises and tenons together because they will be locked in by the external parts. Test the fit of the top and bottom pieces, then glue and clamp in place. Check for square, and don't clamp so hard that the sides flex.

7 MAKE THE BACK

Belt sand the outside of the cabinet to smooth the joints. Glue small stop tabs onto the back of the internal parts to limit the travel of the drawers. Cut out a piece of ¼" plywood to fit inside the outer edges of the box sides, and nail in place in the back.

8 MAKE THE FEET

Make feet for the cabinet out of a piece of stock at ¾" × 1" × 24". Cut a bevel onto the piece, then cut it in half. Cut four miters for the two front corners on the table saw with your miter gauge. There is no need to place mitered feet at the rear since they won't be seen. Cut one miter on each end of the two 12" pieces. Next cut the pieces to length with a cutoff box as shown in chapter one, and cut two unmitered pieces for the rear feet. Glue the feet to the bottom of the carcass.

9 FINISH THE BOX

Finish sand the box, and cover it with wipe-on oil or the finish of your choice.

PHOTO 2

Use the mortises themselves to mark out the tenons on the internal parts that will fit the mortises. Carefully keep track of which part is which so they don't get confused.

PHOTO 3

Cut away the waste between the tenons on the table saw with a dado set and a tall fence attached to your miter gauge. Keep your fingers high and your eyes on what you are doing.

PHOTO 4

Fit together all the internal parts, then glue together the outside corner joints.

CHAPTER ELEVEN

Box Joinery: Making Rabbet, Groove and Interlocking Joints

This interlocking joint can be cut on the table saw.

BOX JOINERY OVERVIEW

There are a variety of simple or complicated joints you can cut on your table saw or router table. Use these joints for any box or drawer. Choose which joint you use by considering what look you want, the strength the joint needs, and the tooling you have.

The Rabbet Joint

A simple rabbet helps make a joint significantly stronger than a butt joint with no rabbet, but this will require more than just glue to hold it together. Install finish nails as shown. Predrill for the nails or the wood may split. Cut a rabbet on the table saw or on a router table with a rabbeting cutter.

The Tongue-and-Groove Joint

This joint will be strong enough with glue that you don't need to nail it, but the tongue must fit the groove snugly

for a good glue bond. You can make it with a table saw blade and several passes or with router bits at the router table.

The Locking Miter Joint

Miter joints look the best since all you see is the joint at the corner, with no joints on the faces or exposed end grain. You can make this joint with numerous cuts at the table saw, but it's tricky to line them all up. Many router bit suppliers make a bit that cuts this joint, and the resulting tight fit takes glue well for a strong joint.

The Splined Miter Joint

A simpler miter joint, this one can easily be made on the table saw. Cut the miters with the blade tilted at 45°, then leave the blade at that angle and place the work on the opposite side of the blade. Cut spline grooves as shown. For the splines to be strong, their grain must run across the joint, from slot to slot, not parallel to the joint. If the grain runs parallel to the joint, following the line of the slots, the splines will split when stressed. Make several short splines for long joints, and fit them snugly for a good glue bond.

The Multiple Tongue-and-Groove Interlocking Joint

Let's take a close look at how to make the most complicated of these joints. This interlocking joint has a lot of faces on it, all of which must line up well for a good fit. The reality of making such a joint is that you cannot make it fit absolutely perfectly unless you have a precision milling machine, so cut the joints to fit just a bit loosely. This way, even with slight variations between different cuts on individual parts, the joints will still fit and glue up well. This type of joint leaves plenty of surface area for glue. This will strengthen a joint considerably.

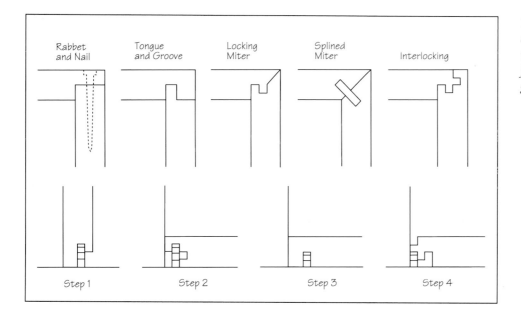

| Rabbet and Nail | Tongue and Groove | Locking Miter | Splined Miter | Interlocking |

| Step 1 | Step 2 | Step 3 | Step 4 |

This drawing shows five types of joints, as well as the steps involved in making the last of the five, the multiple tongue-and-groove interlocking joint.

MAKING DRAWERS FOR THE BOX OF DRAWERS

1 PREPARE THE STOCK

To grain match all the drawer fronts for the box of drawers, first find a wide piece of wood with nice figure. Next draw a full-scale rendition of the box front onto the board, including the drawer fronts and dividers as in photo 1. Mark all the drawer fronts so you can keep them in order. Cut away the divider areas leaving the drawer fronts remaining. It's important for the sake of grain matching to follow this procedure so the figured grain from one drawer front to the next won't appear to be offset by the thickness of a divider or two.

2 MAKE THE DRAWER FRONTS AND REARS

The general approach to use for making such a joint is to make the easiest half of the joint first, then make the other half to fit the first. Make the drawer fronts and rears first, with two cuts as shown in the drawing.

3 SET UP THE SLIDING JIG

To make the first cut safely on the table saw, build the simple sliding jig as shown in photo 2. The jig is simply a toggle clamp attached to a long board that slides along your table saw fence. Attach the toggle clamp to the board with a spacer, which also backs up the cut to avoid tearout. The board clamped to the back of the table saw holds the sliding board in place when you are loading the jig so it won't fall into the blade.

PHOTO 1

To grain match all the drawer fronts, you must carefully mark all the pieces so you can realign them later. Draw the front of the cabinet on your wood, then cut out the areas of the dividers.

PHOTO 2

Cut grooves on the drawer fronts and rears with this sliding jig. Make sure the screws that hold the toggle clamp to the sliding fence are well above where the blade will cut.

PHOTO 3

Make the second groove on the fronts and rears with the part flat on the table. Use an auxiliary fence screwed to the miter gauge for support and safety.

PHOTO 5

Finally make two rabbeting cuts on the ends of the sides to form the small tongue on the very ends of the sides.

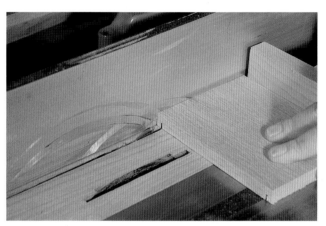

PHOTO 4

Begin the drawer sides with a groove for the tongue on the fronts and rears.

PHOTO 6

Reduce the width of the drawer rears so the bottoms can slide in from behind. Nail the bottoms to the backs.

4 MAKE TEST CUTS

Use test pieces to set up this and all cuts. Set the blade away from the sliding jig at a distance equal to the kerf cut by the blade, and make the cut as shown. The height of the cut must equal the thickness of the sides.

Make the second cut on the drawer fronts and rears with your miter gauge as in photo 3. To do so safely, you must screw a backup fence to the miter gauge as shown. Make the height of this cut about three times the thickness of your saw blade.

5 CUT THE DRAWER SIDES

Begin with the single slot cut as in the drawing and as shown in photo 4. Match the depth of the cut and the distance from the end of the part to the corresponding cuts on the drawer fronts and rears.

6 CUT RABBETS INTO THE SIDES

Finally make the two rabbeting cuts on the very ends of the sides that leave the small central tongue as in the drawing and photo 5. Using your test pieces, adjust the height of cut and distance from the part end to leave a joint that fits loosely enough to slide together with minimal pressure.

7 FINISH CUT THE DRAWER PARTS

Cut a groove for the bottoms in the front and sides, and rip the rears to a lesser width so they extend in width from the top of the drawer to the top of the drawer bottom. Thus, when the drawer is assembled, you can slide the bottoms in from behind and nail them to the rears as in photo 6.

CHAPTER TWELVE

The Splayed Hexagonal Box

■ **WOODS**
California bay/laurel

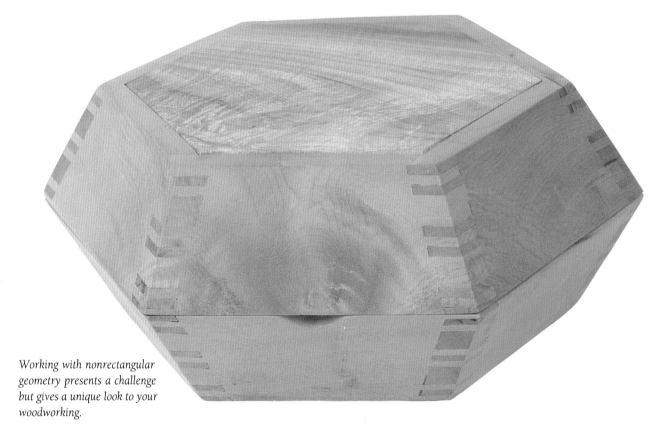

Working with nonrectangular geometry presents a challenge but gives a unique look to your woodworking.

CHALLENGES IN MAKING GEOMETRICALLY COMPLICATED BOXES

I find working with odd geometric configurations one of the more intriquing aspects of woodworking. It presents a challenge because it is more difficult to see how things will line up and cutting the joints is more involved. The challenge is rewarding in itself for the technical accomplishment, and in addition, you get a result that looks quite different from the square regularity of rectangular construction.

There are several major technical difficulties with a box such as this one. The first is figuring the angles involved, which we'll look at here and in chapter twenty-four. Next comes the joinery itself, which is covered in chapters thirteen and elsewhere. Finally, how do you clamp up something that doesn't have parallel surfaces?

WORKING WITH ANGLES

First let's look at the angles. You have three angles to determine: (1) the angle between the horizontal edges and faces of the parts; (2) the angle between the ends and horizontal edges; and (3) the angle between the end edges and the faces of the parts. All three are dependent upon each other, and varying one will alter the others. Note that the last angle, end edges to the faces, does *not* correspond to the angle made by the parts in a top view. For a hexagonal box, this top-view angle is 60°, but the angle on the ends will vary with the other two angles, even while the top-view angle remains at 60°.

Figuring Angles the Easy Way—Test Cuts

There are mathematical formulae you can use to figure the angles needed for such a hexagonal box. I suggest you don't bother with them unless you enjoy such numerical pursuits. It is easier and faster to make test cuts to come up with a combination of angles that will work. Here's how to proceed.

1 DRAW THE ANGLES

Make a top-view drawing of two angles in your box as shown in the drawing and photo 1. For a hexagonal, or six-sided box, this angle is 60°. For an octagonal box (eight sides), the angle is 45°.

2 MAKE TEST PIECES

Next make test pieces close to the dimensions of the box you want to make, and cut whatever angle you want on the horizontal edges of these pieces. I used 30°. Set your table saw blade at 45° and your miter gauge at half the angle that you used for the sides, in this case 15°. Make cuts on the ends of your test pieces with this setup, and then try to fit the joint together as in photo 1.

3 CHECK YOUR WORK

When you align the parts together as in the photo, be sure to hold the leading edges parallel to the line you drew, and hold the bottom horizontal edges flat on the drawing. First determine if the angle of the end edge to the horizontal edge is correct (the miter gauge angle), and ignore the angle of the end edge to the face (which, for the moment, is 45°). Adjust your miter gauge and make test cuts until the end-to-horizontal edge angle lines up with its opposing part as in photo 1. With 30° angles on the horizontal edges, you should end up with close to 15°.

4 REPEAT THE PROCEDURE FOR OTHER ANGLES

Now work on the angle of the end edge to the face. Using 30° and 15° as before, this will come close to 40°. Adjust the angle of your table saw blade until you find the tightest fitting setting. Make notes of the settings you used on your table saw so you can go back and repeat them later.

This procedure presumes that you will use the same angles on all the parts. If you want different angles on different parts, you will vastly complicate the situation. For the sake of simplicity, keep the angles the same.

5 CUT THE JOINERY

Note that the length of your parts will be longer than the sides of the box (when you use finger or dovetail joints). Use a drawing to determine both the length of the box sides and the corresponding shelf side lengths.

6 GLUE UP THE BOX

Glue up the box sides using nylon string as shown in photo 2 (page 40). Use brown glue (urea formaldehyde) because it doesn't grab quickly, which gives you more time to adjust parts as they are clamped. Tape cardboard onto the sharp edges so the string won't damage them. Wrap the string loosely at first so as not to distort the box, then tighter once all sides are held by string. Compare distances between vertices to check that the box is not distorted.

PHOTO 1

Draw an angle, and hold your parts with their bottom edges parallel to the angle lines while checking that the ends of the parts line up correctly.

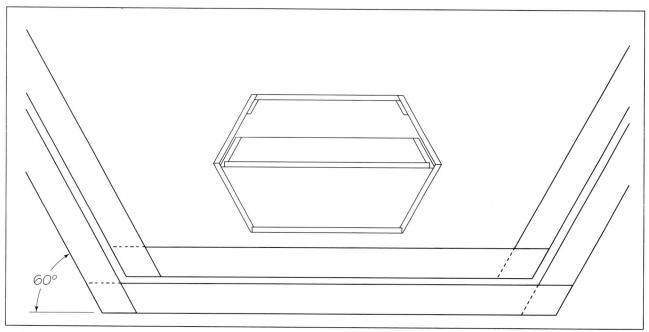

Make a drawing similar to this for use when aligning your angles, as well as for determining the lengths of the parts you will use for the box sides and shelf.

PHOTO 2
Nylon string stretches slightly, so it can be used like a rubber band to pull odd shaped parts together. Once the string is tightly wound around, twist the parts by hand to seat the joints. Compare lengths of opposing vertices as shown to check that the hexagon is not distorted.

7 FINISH SAND THE BOX AND INSTALL THE TOP

Once out of clamps, level the joints with a stationary sander, then scrape or sand smooth. For the top panel, scribe the inside shape of the box lid on a piece of wood, and cut it out at a band or scroll saw at the appropriate angle. Secure the panel in with holders as shown in the drawing.

8 INSTALL THE BOTTOM

Use a ¼″ rabbeting bit at the router table to cut rabbets in the bottom edges of the shelf and box bottom to fit pieces of thin plywood. Scribe the shape onto the plywood, and cut it out to your lines. Nail it in with small finish nails. Include shelf dividers like those in chapter eight if you wish.

CHAPTER THIRTEEN

Making Splayed-and-Staggered Finger Joints

DESIGNING BOXES WITH FINGER JOINERY

By setting up your finger joint jig at angles other than 90°, you can join splayed box sides as shown here, and by adding one step to the basic finger joint procedure, you can stagger the fingers for a less uniform effect. The staggering procedure is not staggering in complexity, but splaying the joint does create some complications that make for a challenging procedure. Conceptualizing what facet of the joint fits where can be a bit confusing, and you must do some hand work to make the joints fit. The result, however, is very unique.

If you have never cut finger joints before, first follow the procedure in chapter nine to cut 90° finger joints to familiarize yourself with the basic idea. Then proceed with test pieces using these procedures before making a box. The practice will serve you well to get tight joints.

FIGURING ANGLES

Your first task is to find a combination of angles that works for the box you wish to make. For this chapter, I'll use the 15°-30°-40° combination arrived at in chapter twelve. You can use any other combination of angles, but be aware that your table saw only tilts to 45°. If you need a greater angle on the ends, you'll need to figure a way to cut this angle.

CUTTING THE FINGERS

1 CUT THE FIRST SET OF JOINTS

You will need to make two separate setups with your miter gauge at the table saw to cut the fingers. Use the first setup to cut one side of each joint and the second to cut the other. Attach the two fences to the miter gauge with a thick block cut at 40° as shown in photo 1. First set up with the fences tilted toward the blade at 40° to the table as in that photo. Set the miter gauge at 15° and the blade at 30°. Make test cuts to ensure that the cut is parallel to the top and bottom edges of the parts.

PHOTO 1

Angle the fences on your miter gauge with an angled block for splayed finger joints. Cut the angle on the block at the table or band saw.

2 CUT THE FINGERS

Test the fit of the fingers using cuts made in step 1. Thus far you have only one half of each joint, so you can't fit these parts to their opposing mates, but you can mesh the fingers together enough on these parts to tell how they fit. Adjust for a slightly loose fit, then cut unstaggered fingers all the way across the ends of these pieces.

3 CUT THE SECOND SET OF JOINTS

Now reverse the block on the miter gauge so it tilts the other way as in photo 2 (page 42), and reverse the miter gauge to 15° the other way. Use test pieces to make fingers that mesh with the first pieces.

PHOTO 2

Cut one side of the joints with the fence tilted toward the blade as in photo 1, and cut the other side of the joints with the fences tilted away as shown here.

PHOTO 3

Use a third fence to stagger the fingers. This additional fence has a tongue set at twice the distance from the blade as the tongue in the base setup.

4 USE ANOTHER FENCE TO STAGGER THE JOINTS

To stagger the fingers, use a third fence as in photo 3. Remove the tongue from fence number two, place the third fence upon it and cut one kerf. Replace the tongue in fence two, place fence three over the tongue, and cut a second kerf in fence three. Now move fence three over once more, and place a second tongue in fence three's kerf that is farthest from the blade. This locates a tongue twice the distance from the blade as the tongue on fence two. Wherever you want to stagger the fingers, place fence three on the jig, and use it to align the cut on your parts as in photo 3. It simply causes the jig to skip one kerf on the part being cut.

5 MAKE FINISH CUTS TO FIT THE JOINTS

The joints produced will appear as in photo 4. They don't fit yet for two reasons: First, you must chop out extra fingers on opposing pieces wherever a large finger was

PHOTO 4

The resulting joints will appear like so. The fingers marked X must be removed for the joint to come together, and the kerfs must be extended to the scribed lines.

left by the staggering procedure. Second, note that the blade leaves an angled cut at the top of each kerf, and this angle must be brought to the angle at which the parts join. You could do this with a band saw, using special fences as you did at the table saw and using a stop fence to limit the depth of cut; or use the following hand procedure.

6 FIT THE FACES AND REMOVE UNWANTED FINGERS

Scribe a line across the ends of the cuts on both sides of each part as shown in photo 4. Use a handsaw to extend the faces of the tongues to the line as in photo 5. Finally, use chisels to remove the unwanted fingers and to extend the kerfs to your scribed line as in photo 6. You will need a ⅛" chisel to get between fingers made with an ordinary carbide blade. Not having such a chisel, I ground down an old cheapy just for the purpose. The chisel edges must be beveled to fit.

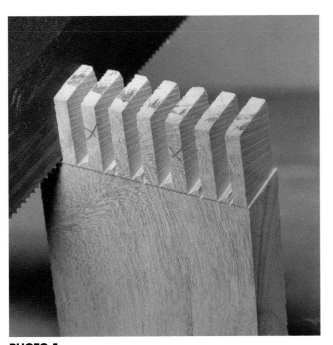

PHOTO 5
Use a handsaw to extend the faces of the fingers to scribed lines. Make lines on both sides of the parts, and look carefully on both sides to ensure that you don't cut too far.

PHOTO 6
Use a skinny chisel to clear out the waste between the fingers. Use chisels to remove unwanted fingers as well.

Stackable Compact Disc Storage Cases

■ **WOODS**
black walnut

This CD case is very handy for organizing a growing collection of modern recordings. The fold-down doors also function as tables to hold the cases while you use them.

STORAGE FEATURES

For those of us who remember when 78s were still in common use, the compact disc seems like something from the interplanetary supermarket. But they are the going thing these days, and many people are beginning to acquire large collections. This CD case is designed to hold a large number behind glass where the dust won't get at them. The case is sectional, which means that if you get more than the ninety-four CDs held in the two sections shown, you can build more sections and stack them atop one another. The sections aren't fixed together; the top fits on unglued dowels placed in the bottom to hold the two together.

Another feature of this design is the stopping doors that open downward only until they reach the horizontal plane and then stop in that position to act as a shelf to hold whatever recordings are being used at the moment. The design provides for carefully located hinge pins on the doors that cause the door bottom to contact the case bottom and thus stopping it at the right spot.

MAKING THE CD CASE

1 PREPARE THE STOCK

Begin the project by getting out your stock. To get the widths involved, you may need to edge glue boards together; otherwise plane your stock to the thicknesses shown on the cutting list. The thicknesses are important in order for all dimensions to line up, so get them exact. Then rip the parts to width and cut to length.

2 CUT THE SLOTS

Cut the slots into which the CDs fit with a dado set on the table saw, but before you set up for this, make four spacers at ⅛″ × ½″ × 5″. Tape these spacers onto the ends

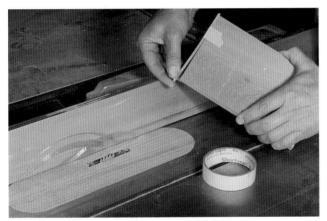

PHOTO 1
Tape ⅛″-wide strips to the bottom ends of the outer shelf pieces so they can be run on the same dado setups as the middle shelf pieces, which are longer.

of the outer shelf pieces as in photo 1. This effectively makes the distance from the bottom of these pieces to the slots the same as on the middle pieces. The middle pieces are longer than the outers by ⅛″ both top and bottom where they fit into dadoes. By taping the spacers onto the outer pieces, you can use the same setups for cutting the CD slots on the outer and middle pieces.

3 CUT THE DADOES IN THE SHELF SECTIONS

Set up the dado cutter at ⁷⁄₁₆″ wide. (I have yet to see a plastic CD box that is thicker than this, but you had best check your collection just in case.) Set the depth of cut at ¼″, and for the first cut, locate the rip fence at ½″ from the inside of the dado. Cut dadoes on all shelf pieces with this setup as in photo 2, always placing the bottom of each shelf piece against the rip fence. Cut dadoes on both sides of the middle pieces and on only one side on the outer pieces.

Now move the fence ⅝″ away from the cutter, and again cut dadoes, always placing the bottom of each piece against the rip fence. After each set of cuts, again move the fence another ⅝″ away from the dado for the next cut, and continue until you have made 12 dadoes on each side of the shelf pieces. Measure carefully each time you move the rip fence so you do not progressively add or subtract more or less than ⅝″, thereby altering the location of the final dado. Most rip fences have a measuring gauge; use this to add the ⅝″ each time.

As you make these cuts, keep your fingers to one or the other side of the blade; never pass your hand directly over the blade. Keep the end of the shelf piece firmly against the rip fence during the cut.

PHOTO 2
Use a backup block behind the shelf pieces as you cut dadoes to hold CDs. Do not pass your fingers directly over the blade.

4 CUT DADOES FOR THE SHELF PIECES

Set up to cut the dadoes in the top and bottom plates for the middle shelf pieces as in photo 3. Set the dado cutter at ¾″ wide, with a depth cut of ⅛″. Carefully locate these dadoes so there is 4⁹⁄₁₆″ between each shelf piece. Make the first cut in the center of each top and bottom using the miter fence as a guide and the rip fence to locate the cut. Then move the rip fence in until the next cut will be 4⁹⁄₁₆″ from the center dado. Use this setting to cut both outer dadoes. Note that the distance from the outer dado to the end of the piece is greater than 4⁹⁄₁₆″ by ½″ because there is no dado cut for the outer shelf pieces.

5 CUT THE RABBETS FOR THE BACK

Cut a ¼″ × ¼″ rabbet along the rear inside edge of the top and bottom pieces using the dado set as it is from the shelf dado operation. Set the rip fence at ¼″ from the inside of the dado, and set the dado height to ¼″. Make the cut with the parts on edge with the outer face against the fence.

6 BORE HOLES FOR THE DOOR PINS

Bore ¼″ holes in the side pieces for the door hinge pins. These must be located carefully, so it is best to do so with a drill press setup as in photo 4. Locate the holes ⅜″ from the front edge of each piece with a fence clamped on the drill press table. Locate the holes at ⁹⁄₁₆″ from the bottom of each piece with a stop block clamped to the fence as shown in the photo. The stop block must be moved to the other side of the bit when boring holes for opposing side pieces. Bore the holes ⅜″ deep. Use scrap pieces to confirm the location of the holes on each setup before you cut the actual pieces.

7 BORE HOLES TO STACK CASES

Bore holes in the top and bottom of the sides for dowels that will attach the two cases together. These holes only need to be drilled where two cases join, of course. Center them along the thickness of the pieces and locate them 1″ from the front and rear edges.

8 GLUE UP THE SIDES

Glue the outer shelf pieces onto the sides as in photo 5. Carefully locate them at ½″ from the bottom of the sides and ¼″ in from the rear. There should be ½″ both top and bottom from the end of each shelf to the end of each

PHOTO 3
Cut dadoes in the top and bottom pieces to fit the middle shelf pieces. Use the miter gauge to help guide the pieces through the cut.

PHOTO 4
Carefully locate the holes for the hinge pins with a drill press setup using a fence and stop block.

PHOTO 5
Glue the outer shelf pieces to the sides. They must be located at ½″ from the top and bottom of the sides and ¼″ from the rear.

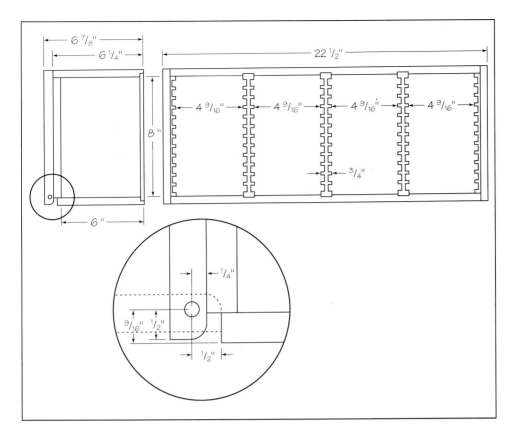

In order for the folding door to operate correctly, you must carefully locate the hinge holes and the front edge of the case bottom.

side. This ½″ forms a rabbet into which the top and bottom plates fit. The ¼″ at the rear forms the rabbet into which the rear plywood plate fits. Remember that the outer shelf pieces have bottoms and tops, and be sure to locate the bottoms at the bottom of the sides. The only feature that distinguishes the bottom of the sides is the hinge pin holes.

9 MAKE THE DOORS

Make glazed doors using one of the two methods described in the next chapter. If you use cope-and-stick router bits, you will need to use ¾″-thick stock for the doors. In this case, follow all instructions and dimensions as given, centering the hinge pin holes on the doors. However, put a ⅜″ roundover on the inside bottom edge of the doors rather than a ¼″ as you would for the ½″-thick doors. Also, you may need to put a bevel on the outside edge of the door bottoms, so that they clear the base or other case beneath as they are opened.

10 MAKE THE HINGE PINS

Cut hinge pins out of ¼″ bolts with a hacksaw to a length of ¾″. Place these in the holes in the doors, and dry assemble the case. Be sure the bottoms of the middle shelf pieces are down. Place a bar clamp across the case

CUTTING LIST—STACKABLE COMPACT DISC STORAGE CASES

QUANTITY	DIMENSIONS (IN INCHES)	PART
4	½ × 6⅞ × 9	sides
2	½ × 6¼ × 21½	top plates
2	½ × 6 × 21½	bottom plates
4	½ × 1¼ × 19⅞	door rails
4	½ × 1½ × 8⅞	door stiles
4	½ × 5½ × 8	outer shelf pieces
6	¾ × 5½ × 8¼	middle shelf pieces
2	¾ × 2 × 25	base pieces
2	¾ × 2 × 9½	base pieces
2	½ × 1 × 22½	top pieces
2	½ × 1 × 6⅞	top pieces
2	¼ × 8½ × 21½	plywood backs

from side to side to hold the case together, and test the opening of the door. The rounded bottom edge of the door should just miss the front edge of the bottom plate as the door is opened, and then the bottom edge of the door should contact the front edge of the bottom plate as the door reaches the horizontal plane. Make any necessary adjustments, then glue the joints and clamp up again. Again test the door operation, and note that you can slide the bottom plate forward or rearward slightly to alter the operation of the door. When all is to your liking, drill for screws through the sides into the top and bottom. Sink the screws, remove the bar clamps, and plug the holes with wooden plugs of the same kind of wood.

11 SECURE THE SHELF PIECES AND THE BACK

The middle shelf pieces should be secure, as they will be if their dadoes are snug, but if they are loose, secure these pieces with ½" finish nails from the outside of the top and bottom. Carefully center these nails on the shelf pieces. Use the same nails to nail in the plywood backs.

12 MAKE THE BASE

Miter the base pieces so their final lengths are 7⅞" and 23½". Use a dowel jig to locate dowels to join these pieces as in photo 6. Glue up the base frame, and when dry, screw it to the bottom of one of the two cases. Center the base on the case so it extends beyond the outside of the case ½" all the way around.

13 MAKE THE TOP

Miter the top pieces at lengths that will flush them to the outer perimeter of the case, and glue and nail them to the top of the other case.

14 INSTALL HARDWARE

Choose a latch for the doors that is small and doesn't have a lot of resistance to closing. Your local hardware store has a variety of kitchen cabinet latches to choose from.

PHOTO 6
Round over the leading edge of the base pieces, cut miters for the corners, and join the miters with dowels. Bore the dowel holes with a dowel jig as shown.

15 FINISH THE CASE

It's a good idea to finish the case before you put the glass in to prevent any finish getting on the glass. Measure the exact size of the hole in the doors for the glass and cut the glass (or have it cut) at ¹⁄₁₆" less on each dimension so it will fit. Use "single strength" window glass, which is ¹⁄₁₆" thick. Make wooden stops at ³⁄₁₆" × ⁵⁄₁₆" to hold in the glass. Miter these stops at the corners so they fit tightly for a clean look.

Predrill these stops for the ½" finish nails that will hold them in. Use a very skinny bit that is just under the thickness of the nails. If you don't predrill, the stops will probably split. Place the glass in, locate the stops and nail them down.

Glue dowels in the holes in the top of the bottom case. These dowels only need to protrude above the case about ¼". The top case fits on these dowels and shouldn't be glued, though you can if you like. But when you buy that one more CD than the case can hold, you'll want to build another case or two and then you won't be able to stack them together.

CHAPTER FIFTEEN

Making Glazed Doors

GLASS DOORS

There are many different ways to put glass into cabinet doors, but they all do the same basic thing: make a rabbet for the glass to fit into. Here are two approaches, the first using the table saw only and the second with special router bits.

USING THE TABLE SAW

1 CUT SLOT MORTISES IN THE DOOR STILES

Use ½"-thick stock for the CD case doors. Set up a ¼" dado in the table saw to cut the slot mortises in the door stiles as in photo 1. Set the rip fence to ⅛" away from the dado. Set the height of the dado to exactly ¾". Run a piece of scrap stock through the dado to confirm the height of the dado and the distance from the rip fence, then clamp this scrap onto the rip fence as shown to act as a stop for cutting the slot mortises. Locate the stop 1" behind the highest point of cut on the dado. Now cut the slots by pushing the stiles against the fence and into the dado until they hit the stop, then retract the part.

2 CUT A RABBET FOR THE GLASS

Next cut the glass rabbet along the inside edge of the door frame parts with the same dado cutter setup, but remove the stop. Set the rip fence right alongside the dado so a ¼"-wide rabbet will be cut. To keep the blade from rubbing against the fence, clamp a long piece of scrap onto the fence as in photo 2. Set the height of cut to ⅜", and cut the rabbet on all stiles and rails. Use push sticks to guide the short stiles through this cut. Do not pass your hand directly over the dado cutter.

3 CUT TENONS IN THE DOOR RAILS

Cut the tenons on the rail ends using the dado cutter. Set the rip fence at ½" from the outside of the dado, and place the miter fence on the saw set at 90°. The height of the cutter must be ⅛", but set it below that at first, and cut the end of one rail on both sides as in photo 3

PHOTO 1

Cut a mortise in the door stiles with a stopped dado cut as shown.

PHOTO 2

Next cut the glass rabbet into the inside edge of all the door parts with a dado cutter. Place the dado against the rip fence. Clamp a piece of wood to the fence so the blade won't hit the fence itself.

(page 50). Butt the rail end against the rip fence and make a cut, retract, then move the rail ¼" away from the rip fence, and cut once again to complete one face of the tenon. After cutting two faces, try to fit the tenon in a mortise. It will be too large to fit, so raise the blade a hair and cut and fit again. Repeat this until you have a good fit.

4 TRIM THE TENON FACES

Once the thickness is right, however, you will see that the tenon does not go down all the way to the bottom

PHOTO 3
Again use the dado cutter to make the faces of the tenons on the rails. Use your miter gauge to guide the part through the cut. First make the tenon a bit too thick to fit the mortise, then raise the blade and cut again to bring it to the right fit.

PHOTO 4
Cut one tenon face longer than the other so it fits over the lip of the glass rabbet on the stile. The finished joint goes together as shown.

of the mortise because the rabbet lip on the stile is in the way. To make this joint fit, make the tenon face on the outside of the rail ¾" long by setting the rip fence at ¾" from the outside of the dado and taking one more cut on the rail end. This cut relieves the rail just enough to make way for the rabbet lip on the stiles. The finished joint looks like that in photo 4.

5 GLUE UP THE DOORS

Glue up the doors, and pull the stiles onto the rails with bar or pipe clamps. Be sure the rails are flush with the ends of the stiles, and check for square. Then place C-clamps on the joints with clamp blocks to squeeze the mortise walls onto the tenons. Once the C-clamps are in place, the bar clamps can be removed.

6 BORE HOLES IN STILE EDGES

When the doors are out of clamps, bore ¼" holes along the stile edges at ½" from the bottom and ⅜" deep. Center the holes along the width of the parts. Use a dowel jig to locate the holes.

7 ROUND OVER THE DOOR EDGE

Cut a ¼" radius roundover on the inside lower edge of the doors. This relief cut allows the inside corner of the door to pass by the lower plate as the door opens.

USING STILE-AND-RAIL ROUTER BITS

These bits cut a shaped profile around the inside edge of the door frame, unlike the square edge left by the tablesaw method. To do this, the bits must cut two shapes: (1) the molded edge and (2) a negative of that edge for the rail ends to fit over as in photo 6. Though generally these bits are intended to leave a groove for a panel (as

PHOTO 5
When using stile-and-rail router bits, first make the rail cut on the ends of the rails. Use a wide backup piece to stabilize the part while it is cut and to reduce tear-out.

PHOTO 6
To make the profile cut, reconfigure the cutters on the shank to cut the shaped edge and glass rabbet beneath. Use a fence to guide your parts in and out of the cutter. One alternative for joining the parts is loose tenons as shown.

in kitchen cabinet doors), some can be adapted to leave a rabbet for glass. Get a one-part reversible stacking set that is adaptable, which will require that you buy an additional cutter to put on the shank for cutting the rabbet. Experiment with the bits to see how they work and how to get a tight joint with them.

CHAPTER SIXTEEN

The Chinese Puzzle Box

WOODS
alder

This puzzle can be made from stock of any dimensions so long as the parts are square in profile and the cuts are half the part thickness in depth and width.

BUILDING THE PUZZLE

Here's an old idea that's just as fun and baffling now as ever. While the parts are very easy to make on the table saw with a dado set, putting them together can be, well, a mind twister. Rest assured, though, it does go together if you patiently follow the instructions and copy the arrangement of parts shown in the photos.

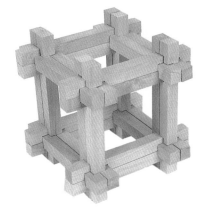

1 MAKE THE BOX

Make the box that fits inside the frame any way you like. I just cut dadoes into the parts and nailed it together, nailing in the bottom too. I cut a shallow rabbet around the underside of the top to fit in around the rim. However you make your box, it must end up with outside dimensions of 4⅛" square and no protruding hinges.

2 MAKE THE DADO CUTS

Notice that there are only four positions for all the dado cuts. The first is ¾" from the end of the part, the second

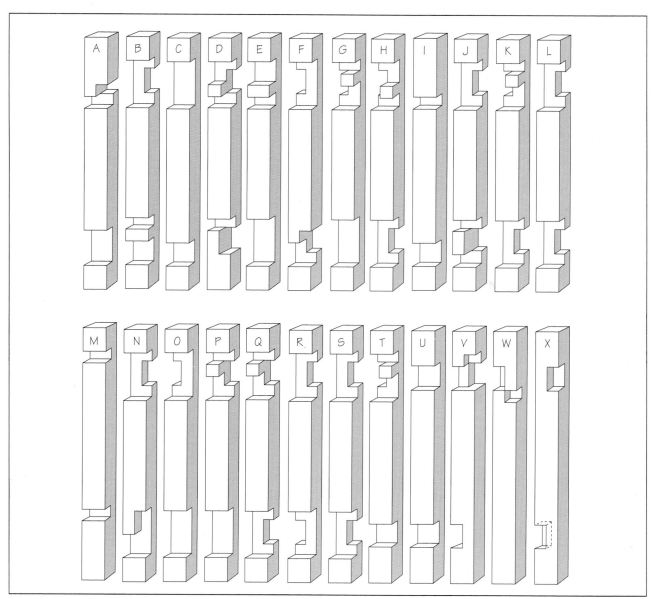

You must be certain that your cuts match those shown. Note that there are four increments of cuts, measured from the part ends. Not all parts get all four cuts, but each increment, where it exists, must be located the same distance from the end on all parts.

is 1⅛″, third 1½″ and last 1⅞″. The end of each piece gets various combinations of these cuts as shown in the drawing. Use this as your bible as you make the cuts: They *must* be properly oriented on each piece for the puzzle to go together.

First cut out twenty-four pieces at ¾″ × ¾″ × 8″ long. Set up the dado at ⅜″ wide and your miter gauge as shown in photo 1, and locate your rip fence at ¾″ from the cutter for the first set of cuts. For the second, however, set the rip fence at just about ¼″ greater than 1⅛″, and make the others progressively larger by that amount too. This additional clearance eliminates binding while the parts are assembled. If you wish, make the cuts exactly on, then increase the cuts with a pocketknife only as

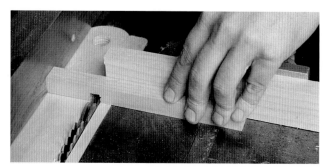

PHOTO 1

Make the dado cuts using your miter gauge as a guide. Screw a support fence to the gauge as shown. Use your rip fence to refer each of the four incremental cuts. Raise the dado cutter to just over half the part thickness.

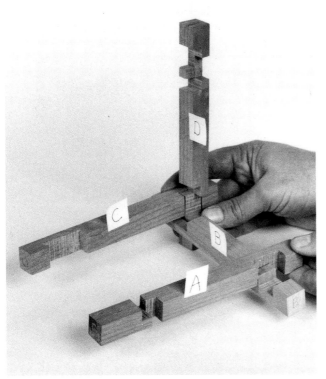

PHOTO 2
Begin with parts A, B, C and D. You will need to hold B, C and D together by hand until more parts are applied.

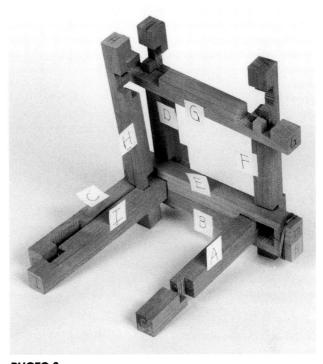

PHOTO 3
Rubber bands around B and E will help hold them together until enough parts are assembled to lock them in place. Note that H must be located so that its center line is on the meeting line of parts C and I.

much as you need to make them fit as you assemble them. This will result in very tight joints but a difficult assembly procedure.

Note that several of the cuts are not through cuts and cannot be made with your dado set as shown. Lay out these cuts by hand, and make them with a hammer and chisel.

3 ASSEMBLE THE PARTS

The parts go together in alphabetical order. Be very careful that the facets are pointed the correct way on each piece as it is placed on the others by referring to the instructions and photos.

Begin with parts A, B, C and D, putting them together as shown in photo 2. C's small rabbet straddles D. Now add E on top of B as in photo 3, and note that they mirror each other where A intersects. Place F and G on board as in photo 3. F's nonsymmetrical dadoes go up and intersect G.

Put H and I together, and place them on C. Slide I into the hole in B and E until H contacts D. H fits in the small dado in I, and the upper ends of D and H mirror each other. Fit J into the square hole in C and I, and slide it toward H as in photo 4. Place K onto A, then fit

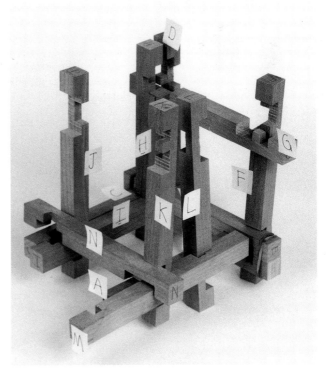

PHOTO 4
Part N will not slide into place over A and M until M, K and L are lifted ⅜". For this to happen, M cannot yet be inserted into B and E. Part J and its connected parts must be retracted as well.

L onto the dado on M that is farther from the end. This done, place the two of them together onto A, but don't yet slide M into the hole in B and E.

Part N is a tricky one. To put it in place, you must shift C, D and J outward slightly so D and H part ⅜″ or so, and simultaneously lift K and M so N can move laterally into place in K. Then N drops down into A. Note that it's the cut you had to make with a chisel on N that fits into A.

Bring D and H back together, but don't yet slide M into the hole in B and E. Now place O under N as in photo 5. The end of O with dadoes going two directions goes under C and I, not A and M. O slides into dadoes in both J and K and stays securely in place. Place P on J and K, its more faceted end at J with the square finger pointing down. Q fits on M, more faceted end up toward P and square finger pointing toward P. Now slide M into B and E, bringing Q into contact with K.

Fit R across and outside of FL and KQ, small dado facing up at FL and down at KQ as in photo 6. To do so, place R above G and below P. Place S across and outside of DH and J, small dadoes facing up with S located above G and below P. Now place T beneath P, with its more faceted end toward J and this faceted end mirroring that of P.

At this point, place your box in the frame. Place U between DH and FL, dadoes down, until the dadoes on U and G align near DH. Place V between DH and J, with the single dado up and at the DH end. Adjust V so the hole it makes with S at J is square, and drop W in this hole with the no-dado end down. Orient the larger of the two chisel-cut dadoes at the top of W facing outward

PHOTO 5

With N in place, return J to its position, then put O, P and Q in place. Now slide M, along with Q, into place.

and toward V on the right.

One more piece! Pull U until the hole it makes with G is square. Lift S as far as it will go, and pull T until the hole it makes with P is square. In goes X, and at this point, you can see how it must be oriented before T slides in, S drops down and U slides in, completing the puzzle.

PHOTO 6

Pieces R and S are the only parts of the puzzle that must be fitted in at slight angles and may require some whittling on the joints in order to fit.

CHAPTER SEVENTEEN

Installing Music Movements

MAKING MUSICAL BOXES

You can easily make your box musical by installing a windup music movement like the one shown here. It's really very simple, but there are a few things to consider.

A wide variety of music movements are available. They vary in cost from less than $5 to—hold your breath—$200. The range of songs available is wide too—from pop to classics. See the suppliers list in the back for addresses.

But they all must do two things: (1) make music and (2) stop making music. They all have some sort of lever or button that must be pressed to stop the music and released to start it. This can be as simple as the lever attached to the box as shown in the photo on the right. But if you don't want that lever exposed, or if the music movement will be hidden, you need another method. Try this: Before you glue up your box, bore a ⅛″ hole into the side of your box body from the top edge, where the lid contacts. On the inside of the box, farther down, bore a larger, shallow hole at the end of the first with a Forstner bit. Cut a nail to size to fit in the first hole and protrude above the top edge of the side. Attach the bottom of the nail to the mechanism's lever with solder, or attach a small block of wood to the lever upon which the nail sits.

To get the most sound out of the box, screw it to a thin piece of solid wood, which may do double duty as the box bottom. This will act as a sound board, making the melody's volume louder.

Try to match your music to the type of box you make and what it will be used for.

CHAPTER EIGHTEEN

Curved Clock Case

WOODS

bird's-eye maple
bird's-eye maple
veneer
plain maple core

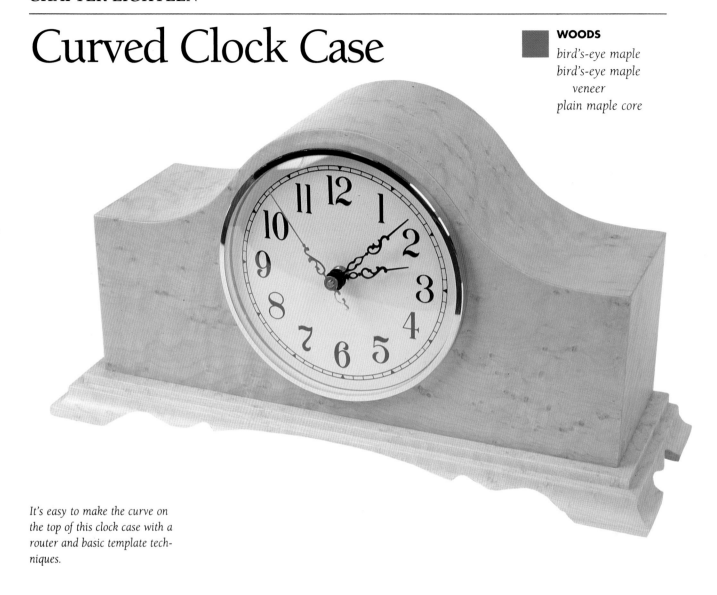

It's easy to make the curve on the top of this clock case with a router and basic template techniques.

MANTEL CLOCKS

I modeled this clock after a beautiful old mantel clock made about seventy years ago. Clocks like that can be expensive due to the cost of the movements, but nowadays inexpensive quartz movements are available that run for a year or so on a small battery. Some of these have electronic chimes. If you prefer, more expensive, high-quality German movements are available with metal chimes.

VENEERING

This project is an excellent place to use veneer. There is no other simple way to end up with a single width of beautifully figured wood along the curve of the top. However, this technique requires that the curve be very smooth and straight across its width. We'll do this with several

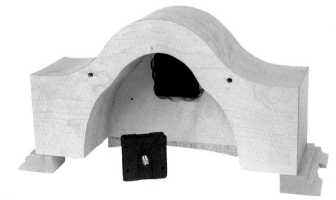

Installing battery-powered movements is as easy as drilling a hole and turning a bolt on the spindle.

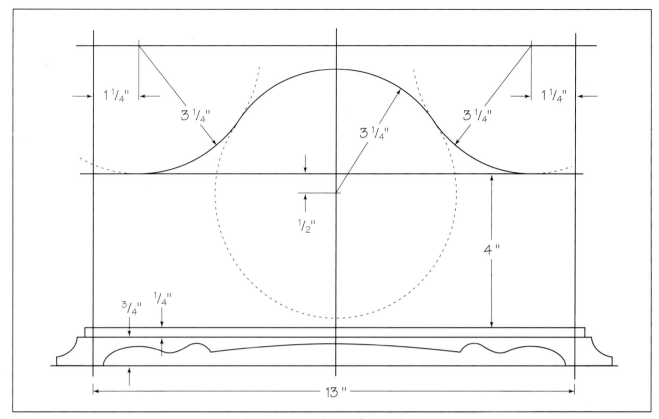

Use these radii, or come up with your own, to make the curve on the top of the clock.

simple router techniques which, if carefully done, will yield a very smooth curve that requires little sanding to prepare it for the veneer gluing stage (covered in the next chapter).

WORKING WITH CURVES

Begin by studying the drawing, and notice that the curve consists of three separate arcs, all of the same radius. They are placed tangentially to each other so the curve flows from one to the other. Our objective will be to make a template to these radii with a router radiusing setup, and then use this template to flush trim duplicate curved pieces for the clock. Then we'll stack laminate these curved duplicates together to make up the body of the clock.

MATERIALS

You can use just about any material for the layers of the body. This is a good place to use up smaller scraps of hardwoods left over from other projects. However, for the template that you use to flush trim these parts, use good quality plywood, such as the "Baltic birch" variety. It is tough, will hold up over repeated use and has few voids. But it is expensive, so you may wish to use something else. Be sure what you use has no voids and is hard enough that the flush trim bearing won't dig into it.

WOODSHOP TIP

Get Your Movement First

As with any hardware, you should have your clock movement in hand before you build the project to be certain that you design the piece such that your chosen movement will fit. See the list of suppliers in the back of the book, get a few catalogs and make your choice. Then as you make the curved parts of this clock case, be sure you leave enough room inside so the movement can be positioned with the spindle correctly located. Be sure you get a face and glass bezel of the correct radius to fit your intended design.

1 MARK OUT THE TEMPLATE

Make your template with a router arcing setup as shown in photo 1 (page 58). Because the arcs are so small, it's best to set up for them at the router table, rather than trying to swing arcs by holding the router by hand. First draw the arcs onto the plywood with a compass to show where to align things and where the centers of the arcs will be.

PHOTO 1

Begin the first arc for the template in a hole in the plywood bored away from the area of the template.

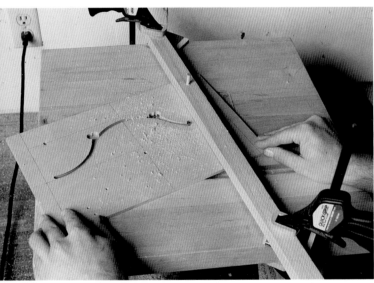

PHOTO 2

Adjust the exact location of the pivot center when cutting the second two arcs so these cuts are tangential to the other arcs at the point of intersection.

2 CUT OUT THE TEMPLATE

Use a piece of plywood that is at least 9″ × 15″. As you make the curved cuts, stay within the piece, and don't let the cuts go out to the edge. This guarantees that the piece will be sturdy as you make the last cut, so it won't fall apart while you work. To start the cuts, bore holes outside of the area of the finished template for the bit to protrude through as you start the machine.

Bore ¼″ pivot holes at the center of the three radii you have drawn on the template. Now mount the template in your router table as shown in photo 1 with a bar across

the top to hold a pivot dowel that fits in the template hole. Measure the distance from the bit to the center of the dowel. Remember that the two outside radii will be cut by the area of the bit farthest from the dowel, whereas the center radius will be cut by the area of the bit closest to the dowel.

3 CUT OUT THE ARCS

First cut one of the two outside radii. If you mismeasured and the radius is not exactly on the drawn line, don't worry. It's more important that the three radii line up than to be at exactly the same radius. Next set up to cut the center radius. Align the bar and pivot dowel so the cut will be even with the first cut where the two radii intersect. Set the template stock in relation to the bit so the bit just brushes the template stock. Hold the plywood down firmly as you start the machine to guarantee that the bit does not grab and rotate the plywood. Keep your fingers as far away from the bit as possible.

With the router on, move the template through the center arc cut until you reach the area where this arc intersects the third arc on the other side. Stop just short of where the intersection will take place, and shut off the router. Your next goal is to locate the third arc such that it will intersect the middle arc for a smooth transition of the curve. Cut away some plywood in this area so you have space for the bit to protrude through, then align it by eye to intersect the middle cut. Now make this final cut as in photo 2.

4 CUT THE STRAIGHT SECTIONS

Complete the template by cutting the small horizontal straight sections on either end of the piece beyond the outer arcs. Cut the sides too so the template is a copy of the front of the clock. Smooth the transition between arcs by sanding, and fill any voids with auto body filler as explained earlier. Bore two ¼″ holes in the template at about 3″ from the ends and ½″ from the top curved surface. These are reference holes that will help align the stacked laminations at the glue-up. Use a drill press to cut these holes to guarantee they are made at 90° to the face of the plywood.

5 PREPARE STOCK FOR LAMINATIONS

Now find your parts for the laminations. You need enough to make a total clock depth of 4″ or so. Make the front and rear layers full size, but the center layers must have voids in them at least large enough to fit the movement. You can use separate pieces on each internal layer for the curve top and straight sides, if you wish.

6 CUT AND TRIM THE FRONT PIECE

Nail the template onto your front piece. Take the piece to the drill press, and using the alignment holes as references, bore ¼″ holes through the template and piece, again at exactly 90°. Band saw the bulk of the waste away from the piece as in photo 3, then flush trim the curve of the top at the router table as in photo 4. Follow this procedure for all the layers. Your center curve layers needn't be as wide as the front and back pieces, but if they aren't, fill in the sides with small scrap.

7 GLUE UP THE PARTS

Dry assemble all the pieces with ¼″ dowels in the alignment holes as in photo 5 to be sure everything lines up nicely. Then glue up the layers as in photo 6 (page 60).

8 SAND ALL OF THE PARTS AND VENEER

Once out of clamps, sand all surfaces with 80-grit to even them out and guarantee they are flat. Use a sanding block on the flat surfaces and crest of the curve, and use a thick dowel to sand the two side curves. The top must be straight along the width. If not perfect, the veneer will still adhere well, but with a glossy finish, you'll see the hills and valleys. Now is the time to make the surfaces flat and straight, not after you apply the veneer. When this is done, apply the veneer as shown in the next chapter.

WOODSHOP TIP

Grain Orientation

Be sure you locate the grain direction of your pieces the same way throughout. If you glue some pieces into the lamination with their grain running at 90° to the other pieces, moisture variations can cause the pieces to delaminate as the cross-grained glue joint is severely stressed.

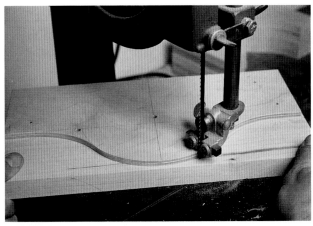

PHOTO 3
Nail the template to each layer, bore alignment holes, and cut away the waste on the band saw. Cut as close to the template as you dare, without risking cutting the template.

PHOTO 4
Flush trim the layers to the template at the router table using a bearing-guided flush trim bit.

PHOTO 5
Dowels in the alignment holes keep all the layers in relation to each other so the curved tops will be flush.

9 MAKE THE BASE PIECE

Make the base pieces with two layers. Directly beneath the body, apply strips ¼″ × ¾″, mitered at the corners and protruding from the body sides ¼″ as shown in the drawing. Glue these onto the bottom of the body. Beneath this, apply three pieces of molding made from stock at ¾″ × 1½″ as shown on the drawing. See the spice box chapter for procedures on making this base piece.

10 INSTALL THE MOVEMENT

Installing the movement is as easy as drilling a hole for the spindle and gluing the face plate onto the case front with contact cement. Do this before applying finish to the wood, or the finish will prevent the cement from adhering. Glass covers come in various styles and attach in different ways, some with screws, some simply with pins that you press into small holes.

WOODSHOP TIP

Messy Glue-Ups

Have lots of hot water and a rag close by to deal with the copious amounts of glue that will squeeze out of a layered glue-up like this. Take a plastic milk carton and cut a hole out of the top, leaving the handle, for a handy water bucket. The hotter the water, the faster it will cut the glue.

CHAPTER NINETEEN

Veneering

There are many different ways to apply veneer. Here contact cement is used to glue it down, with a wallpaper roller used to apply pressure.

VENEERING METHODS

Veneering can be a very cost effective way of using beautiful woods. You'll find that highly figured lumber, such as the bird's-eye maple used on this clock case, is very expensive to buy in ordinary thicknesses. Veneers are expensive too—but much less expensive—and so are often chosen for pieces that will be very visible. Another factor to consider is that highly figured lumber is often difficult to work because the grain is going all over the place, and just about any tool will tear the surface. But with veneer, you do very little finishing on the veneer itself. All your flattening or shaping is done on the substrate, for which you can choose an easily worked wood. Once the veneer is situated in place, you just scrape or

sand, and then you're ready for finish.

There are a variety of methods for gluing veneer to the substrate. Lucky for us the one we'll use on the clock is the easiest of all, but let's look at others so you'll know what's possible. In the old days, hide glue was used with a special hammer to pound the veneer down. Hide glue grabs very quickly, making this possible, but the procedure requires speed and skill because you must work within the time limitations that the glue presents. Some people still practice this method because it does go quickly and is a good way to do repairs on damaged veneers.

Veneer Presses

Another alternative is to make a veneer press. Most of these look like medieval torture devices, with numerous screws mounted in an overhead frame for applying pressure over a broad, flat area. This is a good alternative if you know you will be applying a lot of veneer to many flat panels. But building such a large device for one or two projects is out of the question, and you can't glue curved shapes with a press unless you make special curved forms that fit the contours of the work. These usually aren't used in presses, anyway, because they can be more easily used with bar clamps.

The Vacuum Bag

A similar idea to the press is a vacuum bag. The idea here is to place the substrate with glue and veneer on it into a large vinyl bag, seal it up, apply a vacuum, and let air pressure do the work. The pressure applied is even and strong, and the cost is far less in terms of money and time than building a press. You can make your own bag by gluing together pieces of vinyl and finding a small air pump to evacuate the air. Various manufacturers offer vacuum bags and pumps for sale; some of these are listed in the back of this book.

Glues

With a press or a vacuum bag, you use ordinary woodworking glues. The final and easiest alternative uses contact cement, which bypasses the need for a press or clamp altogether. Because contact cement adheres on contact,

PHOTO 1

Spread the cement as evenly as possible—a bit of a challenge since it has a gooey consistency.

you don't need to apply pressure for an hour or more while it dries. It doesn't have the same ultimate strength as other woodworking glues, but experience has shown that it is more than strong enough to do the job if properly used.

Until recently all contact cements contained highly volatile and noxious solvents that don't cause cancer in laboratory rats. These solvents don't cause cancer in rats because they kill the rats before the rats can get cancer. Seriously, avoid breathing these solvents by using the products in a well-ventilated area, preferably outside. There are now on the market numerous "safe" contact cements, but I suggest you err on the side of caution with these, too, and move the work outside.

USING CONTACT CEMENT

The basic procedure with contact cement is to apply the cement to both surfaces, let it dry, then put the two together. That's right—it adheres *after* it dries. The main problem with contact cement is not having enough on a given area. It soaks into porous woods quickly, so you should always apply two coats, one more if you suspect that a given area has absorbed two coats.

Applying the Cement

Spread the cement with a brush, as in photo 1 or with a roller. Whatever you use, plan to throw it away after you use it because it is nearly impossible to clean the stuff off. And the solvents required to do so are very nasty. Small disposable paint rollers are available at hardware stores, as are cheap brushes.

PHOTO 2

By placing something between the glued pieces as you align them, such as paper or thin strips of wood, you keep them from accidentally touching and sticking.

Positioning the Veneer

Follow the directions on the can for giving the veneer and substrate two coats of goop, and let it dry. Take great care when placing the veneer on the substrate because once the two surfaces with cement contact each other, they will not come apart. For this reason, always cut your veneer oversize so that you don't have to position it exactly to match the edges of the substrate. One way to position the veneer is to place a piece of paper on the substrate, then put the veneer on top of that, cement down. The

paper won't stick to the dried cement because it didn't have wet cement applied to it. Align the veneer, then slip the paper partly out so 10 percent of the veneer contacts the substrate as in photo 2. Press this veneer down hard to lock it in place, then slowly pull the paper out, pressing the veneer down as you go.

Use a wallpaper roller as in photo 3 to press the veneer down onto the substrate. Roll over the entire area with a fair amount of pressure. If you see a bubble of air, poke through the veneer with a pin to let out the air. Trim the edges of a large flat area, such as the front of the clock case, with a router flush trimming bit as in photo 4. Be careful not to damage the veneer the bearing rides upon by applying too much pressure.

APPLYING VENEER ON CURVED SURFACES

To apply veneer on a curved surface, such as the top of the clock case, use the sandwiched paper method described previously to keep the veneer from sticking where you don't want it to while you press it into the curves. Start the veneer on the top, and lay paper on the ends as shown in the beginning photo. Work the veneer onto the substrate with the roller from the top down toward the curves, always keeping the paper just an inch or two ahead of where the veneer is forced down until you get to the ends. Trim the edges of the veneer on the curved top with a small handsaw, and sand flush. Whenever

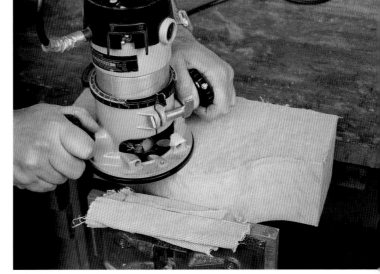

PHOTO 4
Flush trim the edges of the veneer with a router and a bearing-guided flush trim bit.

sanding veneer, be careful not to sand too far, or you'll go through it.

VENEERING THE CLOCK CASE

For this clock case, apply the veneer to the top, then to the sides and the front so the edge of the top and side veneers won't be visible as the clock sits on the mantle.

CHAPTER TWENTY

Nested Boxes

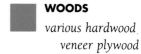

WOODS
various hardwood
veneer plywood

When they are all nested together, the five smaller boxes fit into the sixth. These boxes are a good gag to give as a gift for a few laughs or, better yet, a great way to pop the question by putting a diamond ring at the center.

A BOX IN A BOX

Can you think of a better way to pop the question? She'll think you're a nut by the time she gets to the fourth box, but when she gets to the sixth, you'll be a nut worth marrying. Substitute a piece of candy or a marble for the ring, and you have an excellent gift for a youngster. Whatever you put in the last box, the recipient will have a lot of fun finding it.

1 PREPARING THE STOCK

This is a good project for using up smaller miscellaneous scraps. I used a bunch of pieces of ¼″ hardwood veneer plywood that I just couldn't throw away but were too small for anything else. If you plane or resaw ¾″-thick stock down for this project, be sure to start with pieces at least 18" long for safety while planing or resawing. Bring them down to ¼″ or ⅜″ in thickness. The exact thickness isn't critical.

Make the outside dimensions of the box parts in inch increments. The large box parts are 6″ square, the next

are 5″ square, then 4, 3, etc. First rip your stock to these widths on the table saw. Do this with the blade at 90°, ripping on the long grain on the edges of the stock. Now set up your table saw cutoff box with the blade tilted to 45° to cut the miters on the ends on the parts. Use a toggle clamp to hold the parts in place as you do. This will require moving the clamp halfway through because of the different widths, but safety first.

2 CUT GROOVES ON BOX SIDES FOR BOTTOMS

Use ⅛″ plywood for the box bottoms. You could also use ¼″ plywood if that's all you have, or even stiff cardboard. Cut a groove on the bottom inside edge of the box sides for the bottoms to fit into at the table saw or router table. Note that I didn't even try to do this with the tiny box; I just glued the bottom directly onto the bottom edge of the sides. Locate the groove at least ³⁄₁₆″ above the bottom edge of the sides, and make its width match the thickness of the bottoms. Use a push stick to help guide the parts across the cutter.

3 GLUE UP THE BOX SIDES

To glue the four sides of each box together, first lay them out with tape on three of the four joints as shown in photo 1. Apply glue to the eight mitered edges, place the box bottom in its slot, and fold the box together. Finally, tape together the fourth joint. Be sure that all the corners line up well and that each box is close to square before setting it aside to dry.

4 CUT KEY JOINTS

Cut the dovetail key joints in the box corners with a procedure similar to that shown in chapter five. That procedure involves cutting slots for splines in the miter joints at the table saw, but here you simply use a dovetail bit in the router table as shown in photo 2.

Cut a 45° angle into a piece of lumber at least 1¾″ thick and 18″ long at the table saw. Attach this fence to your router table miter gauge as shown in photo 2 so there is at least 6″ of the fence on either side of the router bit. Raise the bit to a height equal to the width of the miter cuts. Use this setup as shown to cut the slots on the miter joints. You must hold the box firmly on the 45° fence during the cut, or the bit will push it to the side as it cuts.

Do not put your fingers inside the box on the miter joint itself. Always keep your fingers above the height of the bit on the 45° fence and to one or the other side of the bit. When you do the smaller boxes, put your fingers on the box sides that are facing upward. Don't hold the 1″-square box by hand on this jig. Use a toggle clamp to hold it in place if you want to give it dovetail keys, but it's so small it doesn't need the extra joinery.

5 MAKE THE KEYS

Make keys to fit the slots at the router table with the same dovetail bit as shown in photo 3. Start with stock that is slightly thicker than the widest point in the slots, and adjust the location of the router table fence to make the keys fit snugly in the slots. Start with pieces at least 2″ × 12″, then rip the keys off at the table saw with a push stick. Cut them to 1″ long, glue in place, then trim them flush to the box sides with a chisel.

6 MAKE THE TOPS

Make solid lids with rabbets to fit, and drill holes for string handles. These are necessary, since there's no other way to get the boxes out of each other.

PHOTO 1

To glue together each box, first lay out all four sides adjacent to each other as shown, with masking tape attaching them on the outside. Apply glue to the miter joints, place the bottom in its groove, and fold the box together. Tape the last joint together.

PHOTO 2

Attach a 45° block to your miter gauge, and set it on your router table. Use this to steady the box as you push it over a dovetail bit. Keep your fingers out of the path of the bit.

PHOTO 3

Make dovetail pieces that will fit the slots on the boxes with this setup on the router table using the same bit. Rip the dovetailed edges off the stick, cut them into short lengths, and glue into place on the box corners. When dry, trim them flush with a chisel.

CHAPTER TWENTY-ONE

Dovetailed Tool Carrier

WOODS
knotted black walnut

This project is a good place to try out cutting dovetails by hand for the first time. The joints are large and don't have to be perfect because it's a knockabout utilitarian piece.

CUTTING DOVETAILS

I was very apprehensive the first time I tried cutting dovetails. They just looked so hard to make, but I quickly discovered that it wasn't all that difficult, and the few places where I goofed didn't seriously weaken the joints. Still, before you make a nice chest of drawers like the tansu in chapter twenty-three, it's a good idea to practice on a project where looks don't matter. On a tool carrier like this you can have at it without worry about precision. After cutting the four joints on this project you'll be confident enough to try again elsewhere. In the bargain, you'll have a handy carryall to impress your friends with.

The angled sides on this project don't make cutting the dovetails any harder. If all four sides were angled, the resulting splayed joints would be slightly more difficult to lay out, as you'll see in chapter twenty-four. But the short sides on this tool carrier are vertical, and the long sides meet them at 15°, making the angles easy to deal with.

1 PREPARING THE STOCK

I used ⅝"-thick lumber for this carrier, but stock ¾" thick will work fine. I had some knotted walnut around that worked well, but you can use any wood. If you do use knotted lumber, be sure to keep knots and other defects away from the joints.

2 CUT OUT THE PARTS

Cut the angles on the ends of the short sides using your miter gauge set at 15° as in photo 1. Make the length at the top of each piece 15". Then use the table saw to cut 15° angles on the long edges of the long sides as in photo 2. Before making the second of these two cuts on the long sides, place them up against the angled edges of the short sides, and mark the final width of the long sides using the short as reference.

PHOTO 1
Use a miter gauge at the table saw to cut angles on the ends of the short sides.

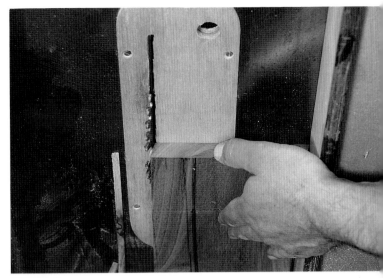

PHOTO 2
Cut corresponding angles onto the edges of the long sides.

3 CUT THE DOVETAILS

Now that you have your sides cut to width and length, you can mark out and cut the dovetails as shown in chapter twenty-two. Before you do so, however, look ahead to chapter twenty-five and see the drawing there regarding laying out dovetails on splayed sides. Choose which of the two design approaches you prefer, and lay out your joints accordingly.

4 LAY OUT THE HANDLE

To scribe the curve of the handle top, I used a garbage can lid, then band sawed it out. Sketch the oval of the handle hole, but keep it at least 1½" away from the top edge of the piece so the short grain on either side of the oval will not be so short as to break under stress. Then bore a hole to pass the blade of your scroll or coping saw through as in photo 3, and cut it out. Use a spokeshave or sandpaper to clean up the curve of the handle top, and then rout a roundover along the edge and in the handle hole.

5 MARK AND CUT THE HANDLE TENONS

The ends of the handle have through tenons fitting in mortises in the short sides. Cutting these mortises and tenons is much like cutting dovetails except easier because it's all rectilinear with no angles to worry about. Mark out the tenons leaving roughly equal spaces between the tenon edge faces and the edges of the handle itself. Cut the tenons, then use them to mark out the mortises as

PHOTO 3
Cut out the oval handle hole with a coping saw or scroll saw.

CUTTING LIST—DOVETAILED TOOL CARRIER

QUANTITY	DIMENSIONS (IN INCHES)	PART
2	¾ × 5½ × 15	short sides
2	¾ × 6 × 30	long sides
1	¾ × 9 × 30	handle piece
1	¾ × 12½ × 29½	bottom panel

PHOTO 4

Use the faces of the tenons on the ends of the handle piece to mark out the mortises for them on the short sides.

PHOTO 5

Bore holes in the mortises, then clean out the waste and square them up with sharp chisels.

in photo 4. Before doing so, however, mark vertical lines on both faces of the short sides spaced at the thickness of the handle piece. These lines establish the sides of the mortises. Then use the tenons to establish the top and bottom of each mortise.

6 CUT MORTISES FOR THE HANDLE

To cut the mortises, first bore through them with a bit the diameter of which is just under the thickness of the handle piece. Then begin chopping out the waste with a chisel as in photo 5. Work your way from the center outward until you reach the lines.

7 CUT GROOVES FOR THE BOTTOM

Cut ¼" grooves in all four sides to accept the lip of the bottom panel. These grooves must be stopped in the short sides or else they will be visible on the ends. Make these stopped grooves on the table saw or with a router table. On the table saw, set up a ¼" dado at ¼" high, with the fence ½" away from the blade. Make marks on the fence at the points where the blade protrudes above the table and where it goes below it. These marks show the farthest extent of the cut.

Place a clamp on the fence for placing the side against when the cut is started as in photo 6. Locate the clamp

PHOTO 6

To make a stopped cut on the short sides for the bottom panel groove, place a clamp on your fence as shown to butt the part against as you lower it onto the cutter. Do not put your fingers directly over the cutter.

so when the part is lowered onto the blade, the back of the blade does not cut the end of the part but stays on the inside face. Start the machine with the part clear of the blade. Butt the end of the part against the clamp as shown in photo 6, and lower it onto the blade. Keep the part firmly against the fence, and do not put your hand directly over the blade.

Push the part forward until the end approaches the mark you made on the fence. Come to within ¼″ of this mark as in photo 7, then hold the part still with one hand and shut off the saw with the other. Let the saw come to a complete stop before lifting off the part. The ends of the stopped grooves show the arc of the dado blade and must be deepened with chisels to match the rest of the groove.

Cut the grooves in the long sides with the dado set at a 15° angle as in photo 8. These cuts do not need to be stopped because the ends will be hidden by the short sides (if you cut the pins in the ends of the long sides as I did). Dry fit the parts together, and measure the opening for the panel. Cut the panel a bit smaller to allow for moisture-related expansion. Cut the ¼″ lip around the perimeter of the panel on the table saw. Note that the shoulder of the panel must have a 15° bevel cut into it to fit into the groove in the long sides.

8 GLUE UP AND FINISH THE BOX

Glue and clamp as in photo 9. You don't need much clamping pressure, just enough to bring the parts together. When dry, flush any uneven joints by sanding, or just leave them as is, in the rough. After all, this is a workhorse, not a parlor poodle. But give it a coat or two of wipe-on oil so the moisture won't affect it badly. Happy tool toting!

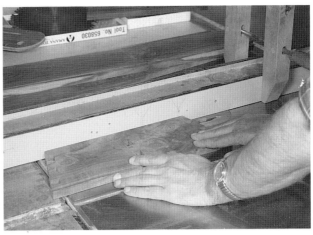

PHOTO 7
Lower the part on the cutter, and push it ahead until it reaches your marked line on the fence, showing where the cutter comes above the table. Hold the part in place, and shut off the saw. Do not remove the part until the blade has stopped.

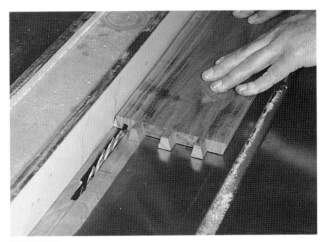

PHOTO 8
Cut an angled groove in the long sides for the bottom panel to fit within.

PHOTO 9
You just need enough clamping pressure to hold the parts together. Tighter clamping won't place more pressure on the glue bond between the dovetail and pin faces.

CHAPTER TWENTY-TWO

Hand-Cut Dovetails

THE DOVETAIL JOINT

Cutting dovetail joints by hand is really not an extremely difficult process and does not require years of experience to do well. It does, however, require years of experience to cut dovetails by hand very quickly and get a tight joint. I'm not that fast at it, and there are usually a few gaps here and there on my joints. But one of the beauties of this joint is that a small gap here or there does not ruin the joint. It will still be plenty strong, and once you glue, sand and finish it, the gaps hardly show.

Patience is what you need when you do this kind of work. Each of the little cuts required to make the joint is easy in itself, but you have a lot of them to cut to make joints on four sides of a box. However, looking at your first set of joints makes it all worthwhile.

Let's look at a little terminology first. The joint is composed of two parts, the dovetails and the pins. The dovetails are the parts that have the angle cut into them on the face of the board and, thus, from the side appear like a bird's tail. From the end, however, they appear as rectangles. The pins appear straight from the side; from the end you see their angles. The pins slide into the mortises between the dovetails.

Note that because of the angle of the dovetails, the pins are mechanically locked into the joint in one direction but not the other. This is particularly useful in drawer work because a drawer front is pulled when it is opened. Always put your pins on the drawer front and dovetails on the drawer sides. On small boxes it doesn't matter which side has the dovetails and which the pins, but it looks nice to have the dovetails on the front because it is seen the most.

Note that you can cut dovetails on sides that meet at any angle or combination of angles. It's really not more difficult to cut the joints on angled pieces, but you need to pay close attention to the orientation of the cuts with respect to the angles. In this chapter, you see joints cut for the tool carrier in the previous chapter, which has two of its four sides angled. These procedures will apply just as they are to joining boxes with all sides at 90° to the horizontal. See chapter twenty-four regarding cutting joints on splayed boxes that have all four sides angled.

1 MARKING OUT THE JOINTS

Begin a joint by carefully marking out the dovetails or pins on one piece, but don't mark the other side yet. When the first is cut out, it will be used to mark out the other. This way you cut the other side of the joint to fit how the first part actually is, not how it's supposed to be. You can do the dovetails or pins first; it doesn't matter.

Let's start with the dovetails here. First scribe a line parallel to the edge of the part at a distance equal to the thickness of the side that joins there. A marking gauge is handy here, but if you don't have one, mark these lines with a straight edge as in photo 1. Make this parallel line on both sides of the part.

It's a good idea to use a scribe to make these lines and all other lines for your joints because the line it makes is finer than that made by a pencil.

2 SCRIBE THE PART WIDTHS

Next scribe on the ends of the part the widths of the dovetails themselves as in photo 2. How wide you make

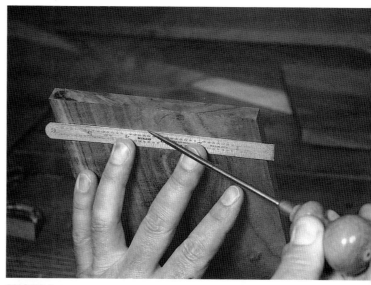

PHOTO 1

Mark the thickness of the joining part onto the faces of the piece that will get dovetails.

PHOTO 2
Mark the dovetail ends on the part end.

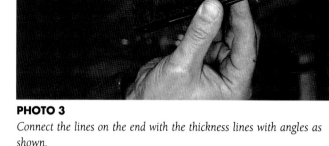

PHOTO 3
Connect the lines on the end with the thickness lines with angles as shown.

them is up to you, but you don't want to make them too narrow, or the base of each dovetail will be so skinny that it isn't strong. The pins, on the other hand, can be very skinny and still be strong. Mark out what you think looks good, and then change it if necessary.

Traditionally the ends of the joints are made with half pins rather than half dovetails since it looks nice to see a discreet number of whole dovetails. But this is an aesthetic point only, and you can end your joints with half dovetails if you wish with no compromise of structural integrity.

3 SCRIBE THE SIDES

Now scribe the angled sides of the dovetails from the marks made on the end to the parallel lines as in photo 3. Use an angle of about 20°. The exact angle isn't critical, but a ratio of approximately 1 to 6 or 7 in the rise to run will give optimum strength. Look at the drawing that shows how dovetails with greater angles have more short grain that can break. But if you make the angles too small, you lose the locking feature of the joint, and you have a finger joint like those in chapter nine.

Use a bevel square to mark out the angles as shown. When these marks are made, you will see how fat or skinny your dovetails actually are, and you can now adjust them if necessary. Make the marks on both sides.

4 MARK THE WASTE

With a pencil make an *X* in the area of waste to be cut out. This is a good idea because it's easy to get confused

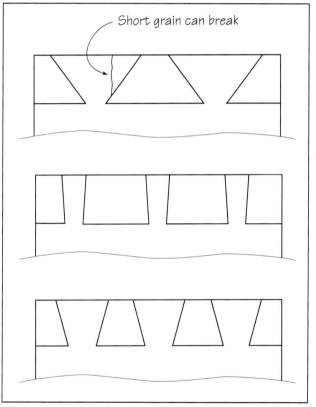

The dovetails on top have large areas with short grain that can easily break. Those in the middle have very little short grain due to the small angle, but the joint has little mechanical strength. The bottom joint is a compromise between the two with dovetails at about 20°. You can use the bottom pattern to make your own template.

about which portion you're trying to cut out and which you're trying to leave.

5 BEGIN CUTTING THE SIDES

Using a fine-tooth dovetail saw, cut on the waste side of each of the angled marks as in photo 4, *not* along the middle of the line. This will actually be critical only when you cut the corresponding pins to fit the dovetails, but you might as well do it now to get in the habit. The better able you are to cut along on one side of a line leaving the center, the better your joints will be. Don't cut past the parallel lines on both sides, but cut right to those lines.

PHOTO 4
Use a fine-tooth dovetail saw to cut the angled faces of the dovetails.

6 CHOP OUT THE WASTE

Make a few cuts within the waste areas to make it easier to chop out the waste. Pull the part out of the vise, lay it flat, and chop out the waste with a sharp chisel and a mallet as in photo 5. Start at the edge of the part, chopping off ⅛″ or so at a time, and work your way in toward the parallel line at the back. This is easier than trying to chop out the whole chunk at once. Don't bang each cut through the bottom. Go about halfway through or more, then flip the part and chop from the other side. This will avoid splitting the bottom surface. Once the waste is chopped out, clean up the surfaces with sharp chisels, and be sure the edges of the dovetails are square to the faces of the part.

7 MARK OUT THE PINS

Now use the dovetails themselves to mark out the pins on the end of one of the other sides as in photo 6. Place the dovetailed side directly on the end of the side to get pins. Scribe the angles of the dovetails onto the part end. Next scribe lines parallel to the edge on the face at a distance equal to the thickness of the joining side, just as you did before. Then connect the scribed lines on the end of the pin piece with the parallel lines, just as before, but this time these lines are at 90° to the edge because they represent the sides of the pins, which are straight, not angled.

PHOTO 5
Chop out the waste between the dovetails with chisels.

PHOTO 6

Use the dovetails to mark out the ends of the pins.

PHOTO 7

Use your dovetail saw to cut waste away on the ends, rather than using chisels, because it's faster.

8 MARK THE WASTE

Again make pencil marks in the waste areas so you know what's waste and what's pin, and use the dovetail saw to cut alongside each line, on the waste side. Now you see the importance of cutting to the waste side of the line rather than right down the line. If you do the latter, you will make the pin too small to fit between its corresponding dovetails. The mark shows where the dovetail begins, so the edge of the saw kerf must be right on the mark, not to one side or the other.

9 CUT ALONG THE PINS

Use your saw to cut out the waste on either side of the end pins as in photo 7. (Note that if you use half pins on the ends of your joints, you cannot do this. In this case, you can cut off the waste on either side of the end dovetails with your handsaw.) Then chop out the waste between pins as before, and clean things up a bit with a chisel.

10 DRY FIT THE JOINT

Fit the parts together. Chances are they won't go together yet, so look carefully along the mating surfaces of the joint to see which areas need to be reduced, and reduce these areas with a chisel. Remove a little and check the fit, then remove some more if needed. Don't remove a lot at once. Slowly work your way at it, and gradually the parts will begin to come together. Trim them until they go together with a minimum of force—a little pushing or tapping but not major banging.

Congratulations! You've cut a dovetail joint. Now you have three more to cut, but don't be discouraged; each one will go faster than the last with your newfound skills. Use the dovetails from the first joint to lay out the dovetails for the next joint, but to ensure a good match, always mark out the pins with the dovetails that will join those pins.

CHAPTER TWENTY-THREE

Tansu

WOODS

curly madrone
alder

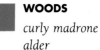

Here's a router project that results in a lot of attractive exposed joinery. If you prefer, you can do most of the joinery by hand.

JAPANESE DESIGN

A tansu is a Japanese small chest of drawers. It is traditionally constructed with hand-tool techniques, but I have adapted my design to use router methods to speed up the process. You'll need to get a dovetail jig for this project—more on that later—or if you choose, you can cut the dovetails by hand. This will take some time since there are twenty-eight joints to cut, but if you accept this challenge, you will become very proficient at fitting these joints by hand. With a router jig, however, you can cut all the joints in an afternoon.

MATERIALS

You'll need a lot of lumber for this project because of all the drawer parts. There is no sense in using expensive wood for the sides and rears of the drawers, so get a secondary wood for this, like alder or poplar. For the carcass and drawer fronts, choose something pretty, like

Dovetail jigs for the router produce tight joints quickly and can be easily mastered by anyone.

Using Template Guides

When using a template guide with any dovetail jig, always hold the router in the same orientation throughout all the cuts. That is, keep the same handle to the left and the same to the right, and don't rotate the machine, just move it back and forth, as well as side to side. Template guides are never perfectly centered around the bit (Murphy's Law #489), but by always keeping the offset in the same orientation, there is no loss in accuracy. Rotate the router, and you will create gaps.

PHOTO 1
Here two alder boards get madrone strips glued to them. On such a glue-up, it is wise to place the thin strips against each other in the middle as shown because if the clamps contact them, they can distort.

the curly madrone I chanced upon and used here (which, unfortunately, is probably difficult to find).

You can reduce the amount of lumber you have to buy for this project by resawing one-by lumber down the middle and using both pieces; you'll get two for the price of one. I started with pieces that were fully 1″ thick and, after planing the resawn pieces, ended up with ⅜″-thick pieces. If all you can find is ¾″-thick stock, resaw this for the drawer parts, and use it at whatever thickness it comes out at (probably ⁵⁄₁₆″ or so). But for the carcass, this is a bit too thin. If you start with ¾″ stock for these pieces, plane them to ½″, or leave them at ¾″. The dovetail jigs will take any thickness below 1″. Note that if you use different thicknesses, you will have to jockey around with some of the dimensions I've given.

1 PREPARE THE STOCK

Use your secondary wood for the spacers between the drawers. Your first step, after resawing and planing, is to glue thin pieces of your primary wood onto the leading edges of the spacers where they are visible. Clamp up such an edge, gluing as in photo 1. When this is out of clamps, rip all your stock to width.

Your pieces need to be cut to length carefully, both in terms of length and squareness. Similar parts, like drawer sides or opposing carcass sides, must be exactly the same length, or the drawers and box will be out of square. Use a radial arm saw with a stop block to ensure that same length pieces are indeed the same, or use a cutoff box on the table saw as in photo 2.

DOVETAIL JIGS

There are three general types of dovetail jigs: (1) those that cut half-blind dovetails only; (2) those that cut through dovetails only; and (3) those that are capable of both. In

PHOTO 2
A table saw cutoff box will give you accurate results.

terms of expense, the first type is generally inexpensive, there are expensive and cheaper alternatives for the second, and those that do both are expensive. A jig that does half-blind dovetails is covered in chapter twenty-eight, and one that will do both kinds is covered in chapter thirty. Here let's look at jigs that do through dovetails only. You can, however, use any dovetail jig for this project, though you will need to shorten dimensions of some pieces if you use half-blind dovetails.

Jigs that cut through dovetails only are very simple to

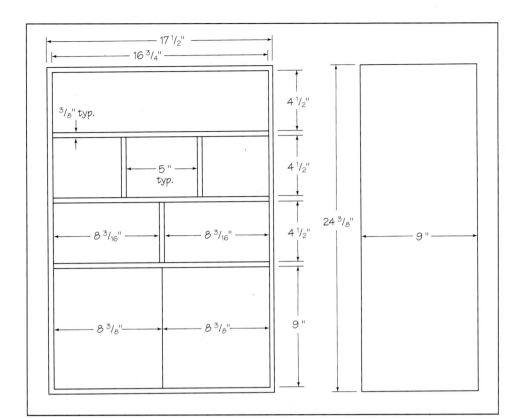

If you use parts of different thickness for the spacers or carcass sides, you will need to alter dimensions accordingly.

use. They consist of one or two flat templates that mount on simple fences. You clamp the template and fence to your work, place your router on top of the template, and the bit makes the cut guided either by bearings or a template guide.

I've found three of these jigs available on the market. The first is the Keller jig, which is precisely machined from thick aluminum plate and uses high-quality router bits guided by bearings. This jig is one of the best quality woodworking jigs I have ever used. Unfortunately, this quality comes at a stiff price.

The Dovemaster jig is made of plastic and uses a template guide rather than bearings on the bits to guide the cut. This will still give you accurate joints if carefully used, but the plastic won't last forever like machined plate aluminum. The cost of the Dovemaster is much lower, though.

The same arrangement is used on an auxiliary template that is part of a combination jig sold by Leichtung. The jig does other things too with its other attachments, is made of aluminum (thinner than the Keller) and uses template guides. The cost is between that of the Keller and Dovemaster.

2 CUT THE DOVETAILS

Before you cut your parts, make test cuts with your jig on scrap until you have the fences adjusted for tight joints.

CUTTING LIST—TANSU

QUANTITY	DIMENSIONS (IN INCHES)	PART
2	$3/8 \times 9 \times 24\,3/8$	sides
2	$3/8 \times 9 \times 17\,1/2$	top and bottom
3	$3/8 \times 8\,3/4 \times 17\,1/8$	spacers
3	$3/8 \times 8\,3/4 \times 4\,7/8$	spacers
2	$3/8 \times 4\,7/16 \times 16\,11/16$	drawer fronts and backs
6	$3/8 \times 4\,7/16 \times 5\,9/32$	drawer fronts and backs
2	$3/8 \times 4\,7/16 \times 8\,1/8$	drawer fronts and backs
12	$3/8 \times 4\,7/16 \times 8\,3/4$	drawer sides
2	$3/4 \times 9 \times 8\,3/8$	doors

$1/4''$ plywood to fit back and drawer bottoms

Then cut out the project pieces. First cut the dovetails as in photo 3, then cut the pins as in photo 4. The reason for this order is that on the pin cut you can adjust the fit of the joint, and if after cutting a few joints you notice the fit getting looser or tighter, you can adjust for the remainder.

A problem with these jigs is that the spacing of the

PHOTO 3

The Dovemaster jig guides your router bit with a template guide. Here the jig is set up to cut the dovetails using a dovetail bit.

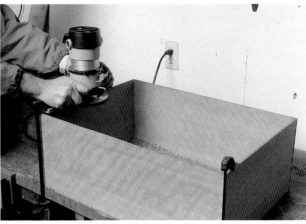

PHOTO 5

Dry clamp the carcass and cut the rabbet for the plywood back with a bearing-guided rabbeting cutter.

PHOTO 4

To cut the pins, a straight flute bit is used. By moving the template forward or backward on the fence, you alter the thickness of the pins. Note the taper of the template tangs.

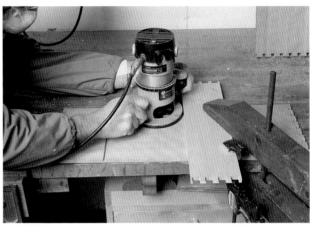

PHOTO 6

Cut dovetail slots on the inside of the carcass sides with your router riding against a fence.

dovetails is set by the templates. This means that depending on the width of your parts, the joint might have a half pin on one end and a half dovetail on the other, or it might end with two half dovetails, which is structurally fine but a faux pas to traditionalists. You can settle for this, or design the widths of your parts around the spacing of the jig. A third alternative is to center a given number of dovetails along your part width, and then use a hand saw to cut off the half dovetails that remain on the ends. If you do this, be cautious not to make the pin cuts that correspond to the half dovetails that will be cut off.

Note that how deep you make your pin cuts affects the final width of your drawers. Your drawers need some clearance in width but no more than 1/16". Be sure not to give yourself more clearance than you intended with deep pin cuts.

3 DRY FIT THE CARCASS

Once the dovetails are cut, dry assemble the four carcass sides. Use a bearing-guided rabbeting cutter to cut a 1/4" × 1/4" rabbet around the inside of the back of the box as in photo 5. By doing so with the parts assembled, you avoid going through at the ends where it would be visible. Square up the resulting rounded corners with a sharp chisel.

4 CUT SLIDING DOVETAILS

Join the drawer spacers to each other and the carcass sides with sliding dovetails that are 3/16" deep. See chapter thirty-two for making this joint. You may not be able to cut the slots in the carcass sides on a router table as shown there because of their length. In this case, clamp

PHOTO 7
When gluing up the carcass, don't apply any more pressure than is required to bring the joints together, or you may bend the parts. Check the box for square.

a fence to the carcass sides as in photo 6, and push the router by hand along the fence.

If you like, you can cut the dovetail slots through the front edge of the carcass sides, or stop the cuts. In the latter case, you must notch the spacers to fit over the stopped area of the slot.

5 GLUE UP THE CARCASS

Glue up the carcass with the spacers as in photo 7. You really don't need to glue in the spacers so long as the fit is snug; if it's loose, use glue.

6 CUT GROOVES FOR DRAWER BOTTOMS

Cut a ⅛″-deep by ¼″-wide groove on the inside face of the drawer parts for the drawer bottoms; use either a dado cutter on the table saw or a straight flute bit on the router table. Locate the groove in the center of the lowest pin. This will prevent it being visible from the front of the drawer, where the ends of the dovetails are seen. The groove will, however, be visible at the end of the pins on the drawer sides. You'll fill that with wood pieces later, or if you prefer, use stopped grooves on the parts as described in chapter eight.

7 MAKE THE DRAWER BOTTOMS

Make drawer bottoms out of ¼″ plywood to fit within the grooves you've cut. Dry assemble the drawers as in

PHOTO 8
Carefully adjust the size of the drawer bottoms so they are large enough to stay in the groove without being so large that they prevent the drawer from going together.

photo 8 to be sure the bottoms aren't too big, then glue them up. While the glue is wet, place small filler pieces in the exposed drawer grooves on the box sides if you made the drawers with through rather than stopped grooves. Leave these long, and trim them down later. When the glue is dry, flush all the joints by sanding.

8 MAKE THE FEET

Since the box is rather Spartan in design, I decided to keep the feet simple. You may decide to make them more fancy. I simply cut out a curved design as in photo 9, mitered the feet on a disc sander, and glued them in place.

9 MAKE THE DOORS

Use ¾″-thick pieces of wood for the two doors on the box bottom. At this thickness (or perhaps slightly less), they will be strong and stable. Hang them with butt hinges, and install catches to hold them in place.

10 INSTALL HARDWARE

A supplier is listed in the back of the book for obtaining Japanese hardware. I used Japanese pulls on this box, which are very easy to install. They are like cotter pins: You simply insert one end through a hole, and bend the fingers outward inside the drawer.

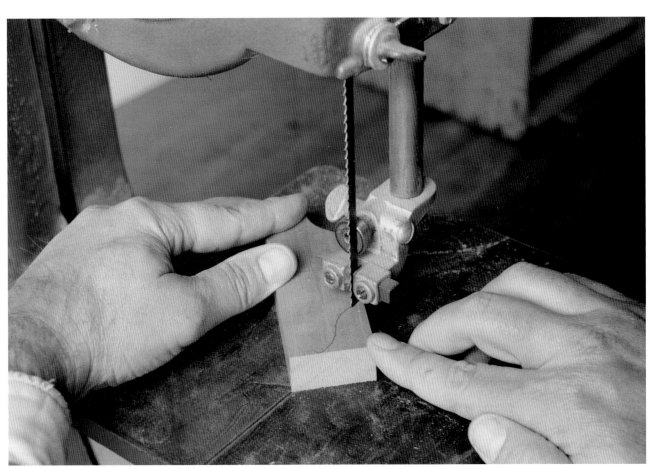

PHOTO 9
Cut the curves on the box feet with a band or scroll saw.

CHAPTER TWENTY-FOUR

Dovetailed Box With Splayed Sides

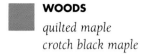

WOODS
quilted maple
crotch black maple

You can make a box with splayed sides by doing a bit of careful drawing and simple geometry. Then use hand-cut dovetails to join the pieces.

MEASURING THE ANGLES

A very intriguing variation on the dovetail joint is done with the sides of the box splayed. Though this may look like it involves technical wizardry, cutting the dovetails is no more difficult than cutting those for a rectilinear box, once you mark it out. But laying out the basic angles for the splayed sides requires a bit of easy geometry and careful drawing since there is no way to measure the exact angles on the edges of splayed parts from a top, end or side view drawing of the piece.

To measure the angles, you must make a drawing of one of the box sides flat on its back. Your top, end and side views don't see it flat; they see it at an angle. To see it flat, you must draw a geometrical projection of a side on the paper, and take your angles from that. It's important to make this drawing as accurate as you can to get accurate angles, so make it twice the size of your actual parts to minimize distortion due to drawing error.

You can avoid this process, if you like, by simply using

You can make a top with splayed sides, too, if you choose, or make one from a thick piece of wood hollowed out with a router setup. Make the shelf shown with a scroll saw.

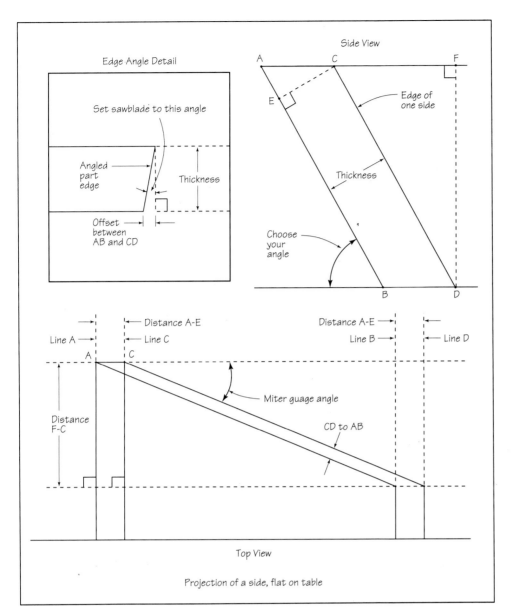

Edge Angle Detail

Set sawblade to this angle

Angled
part
edge

Thickness

Offset
between
AB and CD

Side View

Edge of
one side

Thickness

Choose
your
angle

Distance A-E

Line A

Line C

Distance A-E

Line B

Line D

Distance
F-C

Miter guage angle

CD to AB

Top View

Projection of a side, flat on table

the same angles I did. I made my sides at 15° from the vertical, which meant I needed just under 15° on my miter gauge with my blade tilted at 4°. All these procedures assume that you use the same angle from vertical on all four sides. If you use different angles for various sides, you must make a separate drawing for each side.

DESIGNING YOUR OWN BOX

For you intrepid types, here's how you get to those numbers. Decide what angle you want your sides to be from the vertical, and make a side view of one of those pieces as in the drawing. You can take the angle from the vertical off such a drawing, but not the two angles on the part edge.

Let's use this drawing to give us the information we need to make a drawing of the part flat on the table. First,

we can tell the length of the outside face of the part by measuring the line A-B. Make two parallel lines this distance apart as shown. But when the part lies flat, the inside face is offset from the outside face because the top and bottom edges are angled. Determine exactly how much they are offset by drawing perpendicular line C-E on the side view drawing as shown, measuring A-E and marking that on your projection drawing. Draw C and D lines to the right of A and B lines, respectively, to represent the top and bottom edges of the inside face of the part.

Now draw a perpendicular line from D to the plane of the box top on the side view drawing as shown. Mark this point F, and measure the distance to C. This distance shows how much offset from the vertical there is between the top and bottom edges of the part that intersects the part you drew with points A, B, C and D. This offset is the same for all four sides.

Now make two parallel lines on your projection drawing, both at right angles to the other lines and at distance F-C from each other. Note that where these lines intersect the A, B, C and D lines are the points corresponding to points A, B, C and D in the side view drawing. Draw in lines A-B and C-D as shown.

You are now looking at a top view of the inside face of one of your parts, including one side edge. You could draw in the other edge, but you don't need to. Measure the miter gauge angle as shown with a protractor, and write it down. This is the angle you will set your miter gauge to.

Now measure the distance between lines C-D and A-B. This is the offset from vertical of the top and bottom face edges. The angle between these faces and the edge is not 90°, and you can use the offset to determine the angle of the edge, just like you did to determine the angle of the side.

Draw two parallel lines at the thickness you show on your side view drawing, as shown in "edge angle detail." Draw a perpendicular line between the two, and mark in the offset you measured between A-B and C-D. Draw a line from this point to the top of the perpendicular as shown. This line shows you the exact angle of the edge of the part. This is the angle to which you set your table saw blade.

MAKING THE BOX

1 SET UP YOUR SAW

Use these two angles to set up your miter gauge and saw blade as shown in photo 1. Remember that each side is the full length of the completed box since the dovetails and pins pass through one another to intersect the adjacent plane.

2 CUT OUT PARTS

Cut out your parts, and test the angles you've cut by holding them together next to a square as in photo 2. When lined up to the square, the edge of one part should butt against the inside face of the other with no gaps.

3 MARK AND CUT DOVETAILS

Now mark out and cut your dovetails as shown in the next chapter.

PHOTO 1

Screw a backup piece to your miter gauge to support your parts as you cut the compound miter into the edges.

PHOTO 2

Confirm that the angles are correct by holding parts together as shown and looking for gaps.

4 CUT GROOVES FOR THE BOX BOTTOM

Cut an angled groove on the inside of two opposing sides for the box bottom. Do so in the parts that have the dovetails, and orient the grooves so they fall between the dovetails in the mortises you cut for the pins of the joining sides. Don't cut a corresponding slot in the pin sides, or you'll see it in the pin edges. Custom fit a bottom with tongues to fit the grooves.

5 MAKE THE TOP

Hollow out a thick piece of wood for the top using the router planing jig described in chapter thirty-three. Set it up as in photo 3 with stops clamped to the bars that limit the travel of the router so it leaves a rim as shown. Then shape the top of the lid by cutting a bevel with the table saw and rounding the sharp edges by sanding.

6 MAKE THE SHELF

Use a scroll saw to make a simple shelf. Take a piece of ¾″-thick lumber, and cut angles on the edges to fit inside the box. Sketch a nice pattern in the piece, and cut it out with the scroll saw as in photo 4. Now glue a piece of ⅛″ plywood to the bottom of the shelf. I had some thick bird's-eye maple veneer on hand and used it. It's not terribly strong, but it won't have to support the Hope diamond, so I think it will hold up.

PHOTO 3
Use a router planing jig (see chapter thirty-three) to hollow out a box top as shown. Clamp stops onto the jig to limit the travel of the router so a rim is produced.

PHOTO 4
Make a shelf of ¾″-thick lumber, cut out a nice pattern on the scroll saw, then glue thin stock on the bottom.

CHAPTER TWENTY-FIVE

Cutting Hand Dovetails on a Splayed Joint

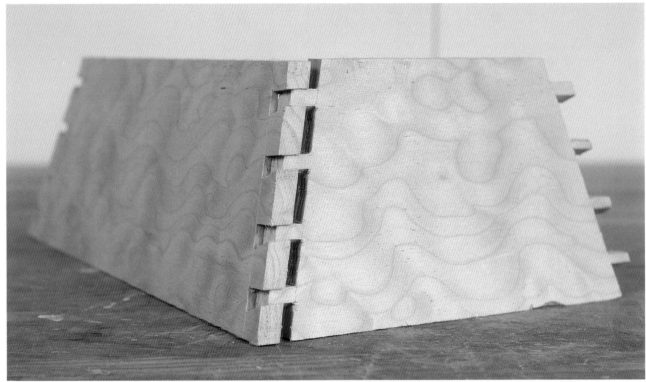

Cutting dovetails by hand on splayed joints is no harder than other dovetails and makes an attractive joint.

LAYING OUT DOVETAIL ANGLES

Hand-cut dovetails on the corners of a splayed box look very intriguing—like a little geometrical puzzle. The actual cutting techniques you use to make these dovetails are the same as those you use to cut dovetails on a box whose sides meet at 90°. However, the splayed angle makes laying out the joint a bit different, and you have slightly different structural considerations to deal with. Overall, the joint is not much more difficult to deal with than 90° dovetails and is uniquely satisfying for its angular appearance.

Begin by deciding what splay angle you want for your box sides, and follow the procedures outlined in chapter twenty-four for laying out the angles and cutting them

at the table saw. Now you have a choice to make as you decide how to lay out the dovetails and pins for your box. Look at the drawing, and compare the two layouts shown there.

A dovetail joint involves a compromise between the angle of the dovetails and the weak short grain produced by the angle. Generally, an angle on the dovetails of between 10° and 20° gives a joint with good interlocking geometry for strength and a minimum of short grain where the dovetail might break under stress.

But note in the drawing that when the dovetail angle is layed out from the edge of a splayed part as in A that one side of the dovetail has a serious short grain problem, whereas the other side has little or no short grain at all.

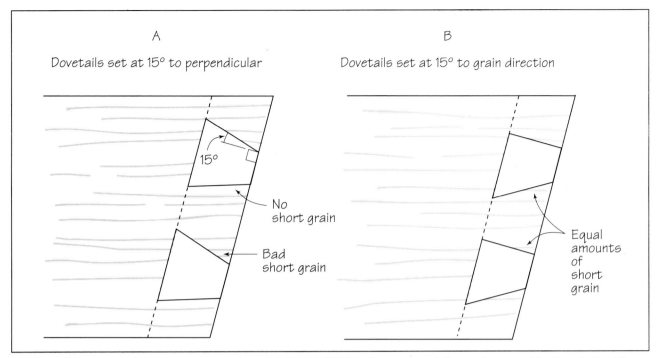

A	B
Dovetails set at 15° to perpendicular	Dovetails set at 15° to grain direction

15°

No short grain

Bad short grain

Equal amounts of short grain

The dovetails in drawing A are not as strong as those in B because they have larger areas of short grain on one side. Those in B, while structurally more ideal, look somewhat odd.

The short grain on one side of the dovetail is weak and could break. We can easily solve the problem by orienting the angle of the dovetail sides to the direction of the grain, rather than to the edge, as shown in B.

But this creates its own problem: The dovetails in B look odd and not well proportioned. For this reason, I chose to make mine as in A, with the angle oriented to the edge, for the sake of appearance. To minimize the short grain situation, I made the angle of the dovetails 10°. Use the layout shown in B if you are making a larger box that will be stressed.

1 MARK THE PARTS

Begin by marking a line on the part faces and away from the edges at the thickness of your parts as shown in photo 1. A marking gauge is very handy for this, but you need to pay special attention to how the gauge rides on the part edge. Since the edge is cut at a slight angle, you want the face of the marking gauge to be flat against the face of the edge so the scribe makes its mark at the proper distance. Make these marks on the inside, outside, top and bottom faces of all eight ends that will be joined.

2 MARK THE ENDS OF THE DOVETAILS

Use a combination square (or T-bevel) to mark the ends of the dovetails on the outer edges of the parts that have

PHOTO 1

Mark the sides of pieces to be joined at the thickness of the adjoining part.

PHOTO 2

Lay out the tops of the dovetails parallel with the top and bottom edges of the sides, using a combination or bevel square.

the groove for the box bottom as shown in photo 2. Make this angle the same as your splay angle so the lines are parallel to the top and bottom edges of your sides. Place one half dovetail below the groove for the box bottom and the next dovetail above the groove as shown. The groove will then be cut out and not visible outside the box.

3 MARK THE SIDES

Now use your square to mark the dovetails on the sides of the parts as shown in photo 3. Be sure your half dovetails at top and bottom are wide enough to be strong—roughly as wide as the parts are thick.

4 MAKE INITIAL CUTS

Cut out the dovetails with a dovetail saw. If you use pencil lines to mark them out like I do, rather than a razor or sharp scribe, keep the saw to one side of the pencil line so you can see where the cut is going as you proceed. What is of most importance at this step is that your cuts are parallel to the top and bottom edges of the parts. If you deviate from the dovetail angle somewhat, that's fine because you can alter the corresponding pin face angle to match. But if the cut is not parallel to the top and bottom, the pin won't slide into its mortise correctly, or there will be large ugly gaps.

PHOTO 3

Mark the sides of your parts at your chosen angle.

PHOTO 4

Use the dovetails to mark out the pin locations. Hold the two pieces together as shown with their ends lined up and the bottom of the pin mortises even with the inside face of the pin piece.

PHOTO 5

Use the pin location lines on the part edge to line up your combination square to mark out the part sides. Make these lines parallel to the top and bottom edges of the sides.

5 CHOP OUT THE WASTE

Once the handsaw cuts are made, chop out the waste between the cuts with a sharp chisel. Carefully locate the chisel on the thickness lines you marked out with the marking gauge. Also use the chisel to clean up the sawn faces of the dovetails and correct any that aren't parallel to the top and bottom edges.

6 MARK THE PINS

Use the dovetails themselves to mark out the locations and angles of the pins on the ends of those parts as shown in photo 4. Use a very sharp pencil or, if you prefer, a razor or sharp scribe. Then get out your combination square again, and transfer the pin angles to the part sides as in photo 5.

7 CUT OUT THE PINS

Again go at the lines with your dovetail saw. Remember that the edge of the line you scribed is the location of the plane you are trying to establish, not the center of the line. Keep the saw to the waste side of the edge of your lines. If anything, cut out the pins a bit too large rather than too small. You can trim them to fit later, but if they are too small, you have no recourse (other than gluing on filler pieces, which you want to avoid).

8 DRY FIT THE DOVETAILS

When you finish cutting, all scribed lines should still be visible. Try to fit the joint together, and see which pins are too big to fit and which are close. Trim the large ones

PHOTO 6

Cut out the pins to the waste side of the lines with a dovetail saw, chop the waste away with a chisel, then trim the pins to fit their mortises.

as in photo 6 with a sharp chisel. Use the trim and fit approach, that is, make one or two small cuts and test the fit before making any more. Gradually bring the parts to size rather than trying to do so quickly, and you will be rewarded with tighter joints. The fit is right when the parts can be pushed together by hand with some pressure but not a lot.

CHAPTER TWENTY-SIX

Oriental Box of Drawers

WOODS
teak
mahogany

This box has a through mortise-and-tenon frame with drawers that slide along the internal edges of the side rails. Wedges, not glue, hold the frame together.

PINNED MORTISE AND TENON JOINERY

Here's a different approach to designing a box. This "box" is really a structure of posts and rails joined with pinned or wedged mortises and tenons. All of the drawer sides are exposed within this structure, and the drawers are supported by it.

If you wish, you can eliminate the curved top rails on this box to simplify its construction. Replace them with straight rails of the same width, and adjust the widths of the front and rear drawer parts for the top drawer accordingly.

1 PREPARE THE STOCK

Determine what stock you will use for your top rail (and top drawer rails, if you grain match), and draw a center line on the stock. This center line is important for locating the relationship of the top drawer curve to the top rail, as well as the location of the mortises in the top rail.

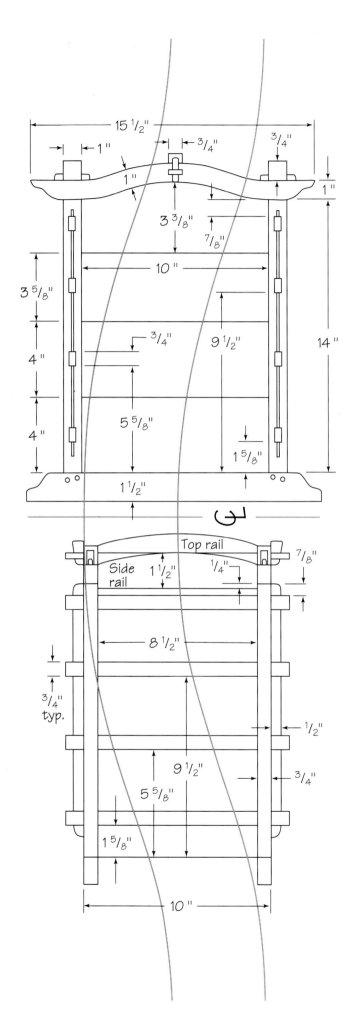

All frame parts (first seven items) are ¾″ thick. The exact length of the drawer sides will depend on the joinery you choose for the drawers.

QUANTITY	DIMENSIONS (IN INCHES)	PART
2	1½ × 16	bottom rails
2	2 × 15½	top rails
4	1 × 16¾	posts
8	1⅜ × 12	side rails
2	1 × 8⅞	corner rails
1	1½ × 12	top center rail
14	¼ × 9	slats
4	¾ × 4 × 10	fronts and backs, drawers 1 and 2
2	¾ × 3⅝ × 10	front and back, drawer 3
2	¾ × 3¼ × 10	front and back, top drawer
4	½ × 4 × 10	drawer sides
2	½ × 3⅝ × 10	drawer sides
2	½ × 2¼ × 10	drawer sides

Use the full-size template (left) of the top rail. Be sure to trace it exactly, using the center line for alignment.

2 MAKE A PATTERN

Trace the outline of the top rail curve onto a piece of thin typing paper directly from the drawing. Be sure to include the center line on your tracing. Align the center line of your tracing onto the center line of your top rail stock as shown in photo 1 (page 90). Cut a hole in the tracing so you can see where the two center lines match up as shown in the photo.

3 MARK OUT THE TOP RAIL

Use a sharp screw to puncture through the tracing onto the wood below, marking on it where the curve goes. Make these punctures exactly on the line of cut. Remove the tracing, and sketch along the punctures with a pencil. Use a ruler to continue the straight sections of the rail at the ends. Measure from the center line to the ends to establish the length of the rail, and hand sketch in the curves on the rail ends.

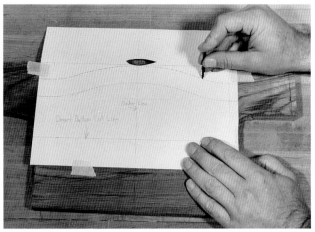

PHOTO 1

Align your tracing to a center line that you drew on your parts, and transfer the curve to the wood with a sharp screw.

PHOTO 2

Cut out the curves on the band saw. Use a ¼" blade, and follow the curve slowly and smoothly.

PHOTO 3

A sharp, curved-soled spokeshave will quickly clean up the marks left by the band saw. Use sandpaper if you prefer.

4 CUT OUT THE RAIL

Cut out the top rail on a band or scroll saw as in photo 2. Note that if you have grain matched the top rail and drawer face, the cut you make between them must be right on the line and must have a smooth curve. Go very slowly, and watch the line of the cut carefully. Cut out the curves on the ends of the top and bottom rails, too.

5 SHAPE THE TOP RAIL

Use a curved base spokeshave to smooth the inside curves on the top rail as in photo 3. You can also use sandpaper with a curved sanding block, such as the back of the rubber sanding blocks commonly available. Remove as little wood as possible on the inside curve so the shape still matches the curve of the top rail. Compare the two frequently so you are sure they still match.

6 SMOOTH THE INSIDE CURVES

Smooth the tight, inside curves on the ends of the rails with a small diameter drum sander mounted in the drill press as in photo 4. These tools are available at most hardware stores. This sander removes the band saw marks and helps smooth out the curve, but it leaves a rough surface. Smooth it out with a scraper as in photo 5.

7 CUT OUT FRAME PARTS

Having finished the curve work on the top and bottom rails, get out all the other frame parts, which, happily, are all straight and easy to make. You will put curves on the edges of the mid-rails that pass between the front and rear frames but not until after cutting the tenons on them at the band saw.

WOODSHOP TIP

Grain Matching

Note that the top rail and two top drawer faces on this box were all cut from the same piece of wood so the grain matches between the three pieces. The same is true of the bottom rail and bottom drawer. Use this technique where you can, if you have stock that is wide enough to begin with. Matching grain shows an attention to detail that is found only in better woodworking.

Using a Curved Base Spokeshave

A curved soled spokeshave is more difficult to use than a flat base spokeshave. This is because it is harder to keep the sole on the wood through the cut, which is necessary for smooth operation. First, be sure the iron is very sharp. Second, use fairly hard pressure to push the tool down onto the wood during the cut. Apply more pressure to keep the tool onto the wood than you apply to move the tool across the wood.

8 CUT MORTISE-AND-TENON JOINTS

Next cut all of the mortises and tenons for the frame components, following the instructions given in the next chapter. Note that all the mid-rails that pass between the front and rear frames have through tenons except the two mid-rails at the top corners. These have short stub tenons that are only 3/16" long. Cut the mortises for these stub tenons into curved top rails before cutting the post mortises in these rails. Make the mortises in the bottom rails 1 1/8" deep and the tenons to fit them 1" long.

9 SHAPE THE RAIL CURVES

After cutting the tenons, shape the outer edges of the mid-rails with gradual curves. First sketch the curve onto the parts with a pencil, but be sure you don't reduce the tenon shoulder dimension so the edge falls below the edge of the top rail or post that the mid-rail intersects. A power sander is handy for shaping the curve as in photo 7 (page 92), or shape it with a spokeshave or block plane. Use a flat base spokeshave to shape outer curves such as these.

10 MAKE THE TOP

Make the box top out of slats that fit into a curved groove cut along the inside edge of both curved top rails. To make this curved groove, set up on the router table with a point location fence and featherboard as shown in photo 8 (page 93). The point location fence is simply a thin piece of wood with a rounded end clamped to the table as shown. Put a 1/4" straight flute bit in the router, and raise it 3/16" above the table. Set the end of the fence at 3/8" from the bit. Clamp a featherboard onto the other side of the bit as shown to apply pressure to the part

PHOTO 4
Mount a small drum sander in the drill press to smooth and shape the curves on the ends of the rails. Be careful not to taper the curve onto the area of the mortise-and-tenon joint, or you will create a gap at the tenon shoulder.

PHOTO 5
Clean up the marks left by the drum sander with a scraper. If the scraper is sharp, it will leave a smooth finish that won't need sanding. Otherwise, it will leave a surface that requires a minimum of sanding.

Using a Scraper

Putting a sharp burr onto a scraper so that it produces tissue shavings and a very smooth surface is hard to do. An easier method is to simply file the scraper edge flat, smooth the edge on fine stones, and use it without a burr. Without a burr it won't work as well or leave as smooth a surface, but it will work well for cleaning up curved edges such as in this project. The finish it leaves will require a minimum of sanding with fine grits.

during the cut and keep it solidly against the fence.

Make fourteen slats at $1/4'' \times {}^{11}/_{16}'' \times 8^{13}/_{16}''$. Rip them out slightly wider than $^{11}/_{16}''$, then use a block plane to evenly reduce their widths until the seven slats fit on either side of the top mid-rail and the top corner rails. Use the block plane to smooth the faces of the slats, too.

11 ASSEMBLE THE FRAME

Assemble the front and rear frames. At the drill press, bore $1/8''$ holes through the bottom rails and post tenons as shown, and push $1/8''$ dowels into these holes. Trim the dowels flush with the rail surface with a chisel. You don't need glue in these joints so long as the dowels are snug.

12 ASSEMBLE THE REST OF THE CABINET

Next assemble the whole frame by installing all the mid-rails and the slats and pulling it all together with clamps. Custom make wedges to fit the other mortises as shown. When making small, thin parts like this on a table saw, always rip out long pieces and then cut them short later; or cut the parts on a band saw, which is safer to use for small parts. Adjust the thickness of a small, short wedge with a block plane.

13 MAKE THE DRAWERS

Make drawers for the cabinet using a simple dovetailing jig as shown in chapter twenty-eight, hand-cut dovetails as in chapter twenty-two, or an interlocking joint as shown in chapter eleven. Note that you must very carefully cut off the ends of the curved top drawer face and rear so the curve of the drawer matches the curve of the rail. For the rear drawer piece, trace the curve of the rail onto the wood, and cut it out on the band or scroll saw.

14 CUT DRAWER GROOVES

Cut grooves in the sides of the drawers as in photo 9. Locate these grooves very carefully since they not only hold each drawer in place but establish the clearance between each drawer. Stop the grooves at $3/4''$ from the front of the drawer, and chisel the end of the groove square.

15 FIT THE DRAWERS

Begin by fitting the bottom drawer in place, measuring from the bottom rail to the mid-rail that holds the drawer. Fit the bottom drawer, then measure for the next from

PHOTO 6

Clean up sawn edges or planer knife marks on straight parts with sharp block plane. This is one place where hand-tool skills will really help you because in one or two quick swipes, you can create a smooth surface that needs no sanding, avoiding a lot of sanding drudgery.

PHOTO 7

A strap or disk sander is handy for shaping outside curves on parts such as the side rails. Clean up the sanding marks with a scraper or hand sanding.

PHOTO 8

To rout a curved groove along a curved piece, you can't use a straight fence. This point location fence (upper portion of photo) keeps the bit a uniform distance from one of the two curved edges. The featherboard (lower portion) keeps the part against the fence.

PHOTO 9

Use a straight flute bit at the router table to cut a groove in the sides of the drawers so they will slide upon the frame rails. Carefully locate the grooves to ensure proper alignment of the drawers.

the top edge of the bottom drawer. Use a block plane to reduce edges where necessary to keep clearances uniform.

16 FINISH THE BOX

Round all sharp corners with fine sandpaper, and give the entire box a couple of coats of wipe-on oil. Applying a film finish on a box like this with numerous tenons and wedges would not look very good because the finish would tend to pool in all those little corners. You want all those corners exposed, so people can see the work you put into it.

PHOTO 10

Hand shape the wedges with chisels, and leave the facets from the chisel cuts on the wedges for a hand-cut look.

WOODSHOP TIP

Use a Block Plane to Smooth Surfaces

When you saw out parts on the table saw, the remaining sawn edges must be cleaned up. You can do so with sandpaper, starting with rough grit and working through several grits to get a smooth surface, or you can clean up the rough edges in one operation with a block plane as in photo 6. A sharp plane leaves a surface that requires no sanding. It will also remove planer knife marks just as quickly. Always plane with, not against, the grain direction to avoid tear-out.

CHAPTER TWENTY-SEVEN

Mortise-and-Tenon Joinery

CHOOSE THE METHOD THAT WORKS FOR YOU

There are a great many ways to cut mortise-and-tenon joints; however, here we will focus on methods for cutting the through mortises required to make the Oriental box in chapter twenty-six. The basic procedure I describe here requires that you have a drill press with a mortising attachment and a band saw, but also described are alternatives to use if you don't have these machines.

MORTISING ATTACHMENTS FOR THE DRILL PRESS

A mortising attachment for the drill press allows you to cut square holes with the machine. This seemingly impossible task is accomplished with a square chisel that surrounds a circular bit as in photo 1. This chisel is attached to the quill of the drill press on a special fitting and moves with the bit. The chisel cuts four square corners around the bit as the bit clears the waste from the hole. A separate fitting attaches to the fence on your drill press table and holds your work down as the chisel is retracted from the hole. Most drill press manufacturers offer chisel mortising attachments for their machines. Be certain to specify the quill diameter when you order. The quill is a round flange just above the chuck that moves up and down with the chuck.

1 MARK OUT THE MORTISES

Use a ⅜″ mortising chisel to cut the mortises for this project. Set up the fence so the holes will be centered within your top and bottom rails. Carefully mark out on those rails exactly where the mortises will be. Make the top rail mortises 1″ wide and the bottom rail mortises ¾″ wide. Note that on the bottom rails, the edge of the mortise is ⅛″ away from the inside edge of the post.

2 CUT THE MORTISES

Place the top and bottom rails onto the drill press as in photo 1, and line up the cuts to your pencil lines. Place a loose piece of hardwood beneath the top rail, and punch

PHOTO 1
A chisel mortising attachment for your drill press lets you cut square holes quickly and easily.

the hole through the rail into the hardwood. Move this piece after each cut, so the chisel always punches through to fresh wood on each cut. This reduces tear-out on the bottom of the hole.

3 CUT POST MORTISES

To cut the mortises in the posts, first cut all four posts to exactly the same length. Then mark out the mortises on only one of the four. Use that one to set up each cut

Using a Chisel Mortiser

Sometimes the chisel gets stuck during the cut, particularly when cutting hardwoods. Rub parafin onto the chisel between cuts to reduce this but only if you will not be gluing the joint, such as with pinned tenons that don't require glue. Otherwise, take the cuts in stages, never cutting in one spot deeper than ¼″ before retracting and cutting the area adjacent the same amount. Be sure the bit has about ¹⁄₃₂″ clearance between it and the chisel, or it can overheat, ruining the chisel's temper.

PHOTO 2
Use an end stop clamped to your setup as shown to make the mortises in the posts. The stop guarantees that the mortises will all be correctly aligned, and it also reduces to one the number of parts you have to mark out.

on the top and bottom of each ¾″ long mortise. Clamp a stop block on the drill press table at the end of the first post, holding it in proper alignment for the cut as in photo 2. Use that same setting to cut the other three.

4 CUT THE TENONS

Cut tenons on the rails and posts on the band saw using a blade that is at least ³⁄₈″ wide and that has fine teeth. A wider blade will not deflect easily, and finer teeth produce a smoother face on the cut. First cut the tenon shoulders using a miter gauge and fences as shown in photo 3. Establish the length of the tenons by the distance between the blade and larger fence. Limit the depth of cut, and thus the width of the tenon shoulder, with a small top fence clamped behind the blade as shown. Note that on the bottom of the posts you must cut shoulders on all four sides of the parts.

Cut the tenon faces by setting up a long fence parallel to the blade as in photo 4. Flip the part between cuts to make opposing faces of the tenons. Note that the thickness of the tenons will be determined by the distance of the fence from the blade. Carefully adjust this setting with test pieces that are the same width as your parts until you get a snug fit in the mortises.

The above procedure centers the tenons along the width of the parts. All side rails get centered tenons, as well as the top corner rails whose tenons are ³⁄₁₆″ long. But the top center rail is offset at ³⁄₈″ from its bottom. Cutting this tenon will require two fence setups, one for each face of the tenon.

5 CUT MORTISES FOR WEDGES

Cut ⅛″-wide mortises in the through tenons for the wedges that will hold them in place. Do so on all the

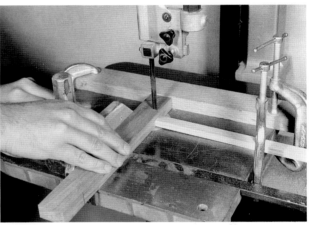

PHOTO 3
Use a miter gauge and fences on the band saw to cut tenon shoulders as shown. The band saw blade guide has been raised for photo clarity. When making cuts, lower the guide to just above the wood.

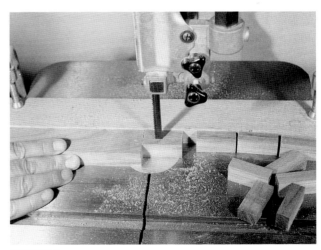

PHOTO 4
Cut the tenon faces by referring to a fence placed parallel to the blade. The band saw blade guide has been raised for photo clarity.

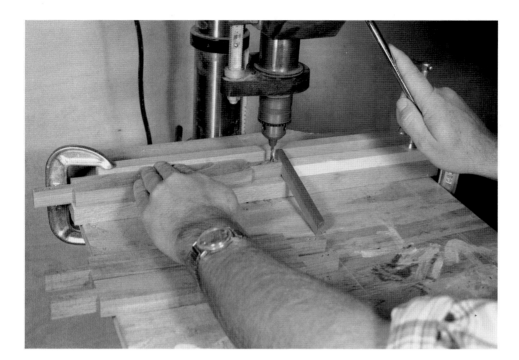

PHOTO 5
Bore the tenons for wedge mortises at the drill press. Use a spacer block between the tenon and an end stop to regulate the distance between holes.

through tenons except the very top mid-rail, which gets a wider wedge. Cut the mortise for this wedge by hand as described later.

6 CUT SMALL MORTISES

Set up on the drill press with a ⅛″ bit to bore holes for the thinner mortises as in photo 5. Bore one hole at each end of the mortises. Use a spacer and a stop block as shown in the photo to bore both holes at one setup. Make the spacer as wide as the distance between the centers of the holes. Bore the first hole with the spacer between the part and stop block as shown, then remove the spacer and bore the second hole with the part butted directly against the stop block.

7 CLEAR OUT THE WASTE

Place the tenon in a vise as in photo 6. It's important to keep it in the vise while clearing the waste in the mortise so you don't split the wood adjacent to the mortise. Use a ¼″ chisel to score the lines between the holes, and then use a nail to pry out the waste. Do the work in stages, alternately using the chisel and then the nail until the waste is cleared and the mortise walls are smooth. Leave the ends round.

HAND-CUT MORTISE-AND-TENON JOINERY

If you don't have a drill press or a band saw, you can still make the joints described using hand methods; how-

PHOTO 6
Put the tenon in a vise while you clear the waste so it doesn't split. Pry out the waste with a nail after scoring the edges with a chisel. Be careful not to dent the end of the mortise.

WOODSHOP TIP

Hand-Cut Mortises

When hand cutting mortises, don't make the cuts that establish the ends of the mortise until the waste in the middle has been removed. The cuts you make in the middle will be rough and inaccurate. Once they are made, you can carefully trim small amounts from the mortise walls to bring them to their completed dimensions.

ever, the work will go more slowly, and you will have to pay very close attention to get accurate joints with few gaps.

Traditionally, mortises were cut with chisels. You marked out the mortise, got a chisel of the same width as your mortise, and began making a series of closely placed cuts within the marked area, gradually deepening the cut. You can speed up the process by first boring holes in the area of the mortise with a dowel jig and an electric drill.

1 MARK OUT THE TENON

Cut your tenons by hand using a marking gauge, fine-tooth handsaw and chisels as in photo 7. First mark out the tenon on all sides of the part using the marking gauge.

2 CUT THE TENONS

Next use the handsaw to cut very close to these lines but always staying just on the side of the waste. How close you come to the line is a function of how risky you like to live. Then come back with a sharp chisel and clean up the sawn surfaces.

PHOTO 7

Cut mortises and tenons by hand by carefully marking out the locations of the faces and walls first with a marking gauge. Then chop mortises with chisels, and cut out tenons with a handsaw. Leave the tenons slightly fat, and pare them down to fit the mortises, or expand the mortises slightly to fit the tenons.

CHAPTER TWENTY-EIGHT

Simple Dovetailing Jigs

MACHINE-CUT DOVETAILS

There are two types of dovetailing jigs for use with a router: (1) inexpensive, simple jigs and (2) expensive, complicated ones. The inexpensive jigs basically make one joint—the half-blind joint pictured here. You can't vary the spacing or size of the dovetails (with some exceptions), nor can you cut through dovetails with them. But they are very easy to use and produce excellent, tight joints if you use them with care. And they don't cost much. They are a good avenue to produce an attractive joint for drawers as shown here or for joining any box parts at 90°

USING THE JIGS

There are a variety of these jigs on the market, and they all work on the same basic principle: You place both sides of the joint in the jig at once, properly aligned to a template that has a row of fingers. You place a certain-size template guide on your router base and a specific dovetail bit in the router, and cut both the pins and the dovetails in one operation as in photo 2.

The fit of the joint is determined by two factors. The first is the depth of cut that the bit is set for. As you lower the bit, the dovetails get wider, but the slots into which they fit do not. Thus you can adjust the width of the dovetails to fit perfectly in the slots.

The other critical aspect of the fit is the forward to rearward location of the template itself. The location of the bottom of the finger grooves determines how deep the slots will be that the dovetails fit into. The location of the ends of the fingers determines how thick the dovetails will be. By moving the template forward or backward, you simultaneously adjust the thickness of the dovetails and depth of the slots so the dovetails fit flush against the ends of the pins, not proud or recessed.

To make these adjustments, you must make test cuts. It is essential when you make your parts to make test pieces at the same time so you can adjust the setup properly before you cut the actual parts. Once parts are cut, it is difficult or impossible to make further adjustments on them. Your test pieces do not have to be the same thickness as your actual parts or even of the same wood; use scraps instead of expensive lumber. (Yes, I know, scraps *are* expensive lumber! But you can't use them for much anything else, so they are good for tests.)

When you load parts into the jig, be very careful to place parts in exactly the same location every time. Misplacing parts in the jig will produce an ill-fitting joint or

PHOTO 1
Simple dovetail jigs cut a half-blind joint as shown. It is called half-blind because you cannot see the joint from one of the two sides, so it is invisible on a closed drawer.

PHOTO 2
The jig holds both the dovetail and pin board inside of it, and both are cut simultaneously with a handheld router.

one with gaps. Read the instructions that come with the jig to understand exactly how it is intended to be used.

The fact that you cannot adjust the spacing between the dovetails causes a problem. If you want drawers or box sides that are of a width that falls between the incremental distance between the dovetails, your joint will end on a half dovetail, which looks a bit odd. You could use the jig to center a limited number of dovetails along the width of the parts, but this creates another problem.

You must cut a groove along the bottom of your drawer sides for the drawer bottom to fit within. So that this groove will not be visible on the end of the drawer front, you must locate a dovetail slot directly over it. Otherwise, the slot will appear on a pin in the joint. So in this case, you must locate the first dovetail as low as possible, which precludes centering a group of dovetails.

One compromise to the situation is to cut off the top half dovetail as in photo 4. If you choose this alternative, be sure not to cut the half slot that this dovetail would fit into. This adds a step to the routing process because after all the desired slots are cut, you must remove the router and retract the pin piece within the jig, and then put the router back on the jig and cut the last dovetail. If you don't retract the pin piece, a slot will be cut where you don't want it as the last dovetail is cut.

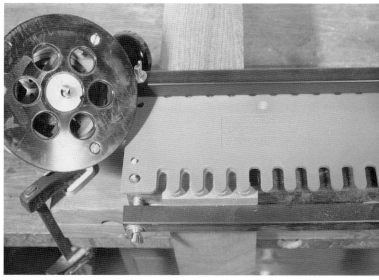

PHOTO 3
The fingers on the template edge determine the spacing between the dovetails. The rest of the jig keeps the boards in proper alignment to the fingers while you make the cut.

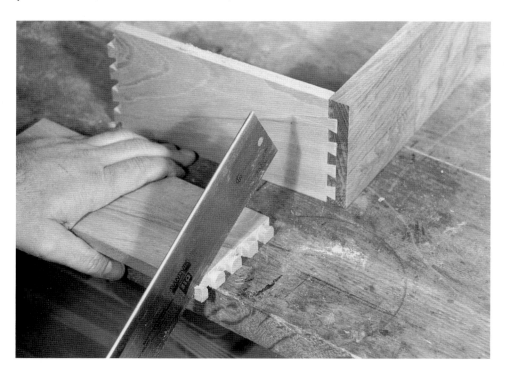

PHOTO 4
Because you can't vary the spacing of the dovetails, you will sometimes end up with a half dovetail on boards of certain widths. One solution is to cut off that half dovetail and not cut the slot for it, resulting in a slightly offset joint that is structurally fine.

CHAPTER TWENTY-NINE

Hope Chest

WOODS
cherry

This chest is a fun exploration into compound angled joinery, and the dovetails are easy to cut with a jig.

MAKING A SIX-BOARD CHEST

In the old days, a fairly common box construction was the six-board chest, which was made from one very long and wide board crosscut into six pieces for the top, bottom and four sides. If you have a lot of 24"-wide pieces of lumber lying around, this is an easy and convenient thing to do. Unfortunately, we don't have much of that left these days.

Of course we could edge glue to get the width. That's fine, but unless you get an excellent grain match, the surfaces look somewhat inconsistent with different grain patterns across the glue line. But it occurred to me that as long as I'm starting with pieces that are not very wide to begin with, I could use their lesser width to my advantage by placing angles at the intersections of the different boards. Now any grain discrepancies are less visible because of the angle separating them.

The odd-angled dovetail joinery on this box is surprisingly easy to accomplish, once you are set up with a jig to do it. However, setting up for this requires that you

Attach rope handles to the shelf to make lifting it out easy.

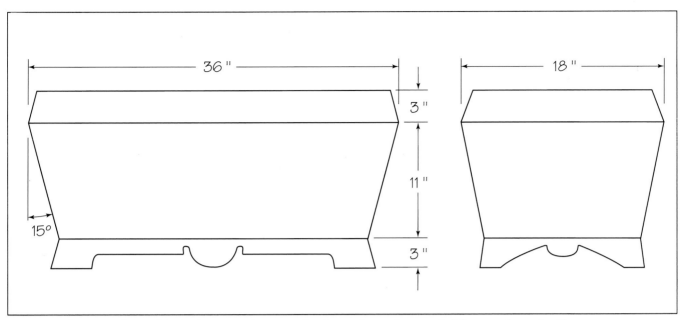

Use whatever angles you like for this project, but notice that the panel sizes change with different angles on the sides.

use the jig in a way that it was not originally designed for. The compound cut on the ends is not at 90° to the face of the stock, and, therefore, the stock must be held to the jig templates at the odd angle, in my case 86°. This is easy to accomplish as you'll see in the next chapter, but the question is, once you have placed your work in the jig at such an odd angle, will the design of the jig allow you to align the templates for a tightly fitting joint? I used a Leigh jig, which does allow this. Others will too, but confirm that a jig will make compound miter dovetails before buying it for this purpose (see the next chapter for more on this).

1 PREPARING THE STOCK

I was able to find a piece of cherry 11½″ wide to use for the widest pieces on the chest. You should be able to find this width in cherry, oak or other hardwoods. But the panels for the shelf, bottom and top are wider than this and require an edge-gluing operation. Straighten and square up the edges to be glued as accurately as possible with a table saw, jointer or jointer plane. You can glue the edges together with no other joinery, such as dowels or biscuits, but these make the glue-up easy because they hold the parts in alignment while you clamp the parts together, which otherwise would slip away from flush because of pressure. Photo 1 (page 102) shows the parts being cut for biscuits with such a machine. Glue up the panels as shown in photo 2 (page 102).

CUTTING LIST—HOPE CHEST

All stock is ¾″ thick except handles.

QUANTITY	DIMENSIONS (IN INCHES)	PART
2	11½ × 36 (approximate)	sides
2	11½ × 18 (approximate)	sides
6	3½ × 36 (approximate)	top, bottom and shelf sides
4	3½ × 18 (approximate)	top, bottom and shelf sides
3	17 × 35	top, bottom and shelf panels
1	2 × 3 × 24	handles

2 FIGURE THE ANGLES FOR THE JOINERY

Study chapter twenty-four to learn about how to figure the angles for splayed joinery, or simply use the angles I did: 15°, 14½° and 4°. The 15° angle is the angle that the faces of all parts make with the vertical, the 14½° angle is the angle you set on your miter gauge when cutting the ends as in photo 3 (page 102), and the 4° angle is the angle to tilt your saw blade to. Note in photo 3 (page 102) that I've screwed a support fence to my miter gauge, which has pieces attached to it that allowed me to screw the work directly to the jig. Locate such

PHOTO 1
Using a biscuit joiner provides a fast and easy way to align the faces of edge glue-ups.

PHOTO 2
Locate your clamps such that the panel is flat. In this case, they all needed to be on one side; more often they are on both sides.

PHOTO 3
You may need to set this up on the other side of your table saw. With the inside face up (for screws), the blade tilts away from the work.

PHOTO 4
Put your band or string clamps close to the ends of the parts so the parts are not bent by the pressure of the clamps.

screws on the inside face of parts. Screwing the pieces to the jig assures an accurate cut. The 4° angle always tilts toward the outside of the part, which is to say that the outside face appears to be smaller than the inside.

3 CUT SIDES TO LENGTH

First cut the wide sides to length, then use them to show you exactly how long to cut the parts for the top, shelf and bottom. Make the shelf so when it sits in the chest, it will lie just below the edges of the sides.

WOODSHOP TIP

Edge Gluing With Dowels

Use a dowel jig to align the holes when using dowels for an edge gluing situation, and keep the holes shallow, no deeper than 1″. When a dowel extends more than that into edge or face grain (rather than end grain) of any board, a cross grain situation is created, which could fail with severe moisture variations. Since the primary function of the dowel is to align the boards for glue-up rather than to create structural integrity, there is no need to risk the structural integrity of the joint with the chance of failure due to long dowels.

WOODSHOP TIP

String Clamps

A workable substitute for band clamps is to wrap many windings of string around the parts. Each winding adds a bit more pressure.

4 CUT DOVETAIL JOINERY

Cut your dovetails according to the instructions in the following chapter. Sketch the curved pattern on the bottom pieces by hand, then cut them out with a scroll or band saw. Gluing angled parts is a trick because bar clamps slide right off the angles. Use band clamps as in photo 4. Use minimal pressure so you don't distort the parts.

5 ASSEMBLE THE TOP, BOTTOM AND SHELF

Cut 15° angles on the panels so they fit in the top, bottom and shelf with their outer face flush to the horizontal edge they reside against. Make the length exact so the panel does not protrude beyond this edge, but make the width ⅛″ less to allow for moisture-related expansion. How do you secure the panels in? Because the parts are angled, the panels cannot get out going one direction. Secure them from going inward with screw blocks on the inside. Attach the bottom to the wide chest sides with biscuits, or simply glue and screw the two together. Apply screws through the bottom into the lower edge of the wide sides.

6 MAKE THE HANDLES

Make the large wooden handles by rough shaping at the table saw and band saw (or hand coping saw) then sanding smooth. Cut a cove under the handle with table saw setup as in photo 5. See chapter thirty-one for an explanation of safety procedures when using this technique. When the cove is cut, cut away other waste with cuts such as that in photo 6. Now take the piece to the band saw to shape it like a drooping leaf. A disk sander helps round the edges, either on a stationary machine or in a hand drill. Finish sand, and screw in place.

PHOTO 5

This unusual setup produces an elliptical cove cut. Make the cut in ¹⁄₁₆″ increments, and always use two fences, a push stick, and no parts under 18″.

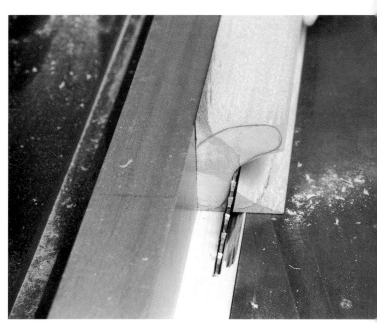

PHOTO 6

Make angle cuts to approximate the outside curves. Then screw the work to a support block on the flat face, clamp the support block in a vise, use a block plane to round the outside curves, and use a scraper or sandpaper to smooth the inside cove.

CHAPTER THIRTY

Using Jigs to Cut Compound Miter Dovetails

Note that the pins on this compound miter dovetail joint are at 90° to the edge of the piece they are on, not parallel to the top and bottom edges. This is a mechanical limitation of the jig that was used to cut the joint.

DOVETAIL JIG CAPABILITIES

There is a wide variety of dovetail jigs on the market, each with its own design peculiarities. They all work on the same basic idea, which is that the jig's templates guide the router for a precise and limited cut. This is done in slightly different ways, with adjustments of differing capabilities. But they all are designed to cut joints for parts that meet at 90°, since 99 percent of all dovetail work falls in this category.

MAKING COMPOUND MITER DOVETAIL JOINTS

To make compound miter dovetail joints in a jig, however, you must hold the piece to the template at an angle slightly off of 90°, because the result of cutting a compound miter on parts is that the end is not at 90° to the faces any longer. The part end must lie flush against the bottom of the template as shown in the drawing. It's easy enough to make special spacers to put onto the jig in order to allow the work to be clamped in at the appropriate angle, but look at the drawing to see what happens when you do so: The angled piece is now farther away from the vertical face that it would lie against for cutting 90° dovetails. This causes the end of the piece being cut to be farther from the jig center line in the case of the drawing shown, or it could be closer if tilted the other way. This is a problem because the position of the end of the part on the template is critical for adjusting the fit of the joints. Therefore, the template must be moved out or in so it is positioned correctly over the end of the part for the right fit. Will the jig allow you to do this? My research indicates this: The jigs that are dedicated to making half-blind dovetails will not let you do this without making serious changes to how the templates are held to the jig, but most other jigs easily allow this to happen.

DOVETAIL JIG ADJUSTABILITY

I used a Leigh jig for making the hope chest of the previous chapter, which is shown here, and this jig easily allows the templates to be positioned as needed for compound miters. The instruction manual that comes with the jig demonstrates this procedure to an extent, but we'll carry it a bit further here. The same idea can be applied to another similar jig, the Omnijig made by Porter Cable, because it too has template alignment features that give you the berth needed. The manual that comes with this jig does not describe the procedure, but that doesn't mean you can't push the envelope of the jig's capabilities.

You can also do this procedure with the Keller and Dovemaster jigs described in chapter twenty-three. If you do so, you will need to make the fences that attach to the templates with the same angle that you have on the end of your parts, and those fences will only be useful for that angle. But such fences are easy to make.

I'll focus here on what you need to do in order to use the Leigh jig to do this procedure, but most of what I cover will apply to doing this on the other jigs as well. Whatever jig you use, make numerous test cuts in scrap until you get a joint that works. Experience is the best teacher.

1 CUT ANGLES ON FACE PIECES

The angled spacer pieces that hold your stock in the jig must be as thin as possible so they do not hold the work too far away from the jig. Begin making these pieces by cutting the 4° angle (or whatever angle you choose) onto the face of your pieces as shown in photo 1. Now begin to cut away the material on the back side of each piece with a series of cuts at the table saw as in photo 2. Make all these cuts at the same height, such that the final thickness of the part at the thinnest part of the bevel will be about 3/16″. Move the table saw fence in toward the blade between cuts to gradually waste away the central area of the piece. Make two cuts at each setting, flipping the part between cuts so the opposite edge contacts the saw fence. As you approach the middle, your cuts will appear as in photo 3 (page 106).

2 SET UP THE JIG

From the drawing, you can see that the outer spacer must have this entire central area removed, so with that piece, continue the process till the center is gone. But for the

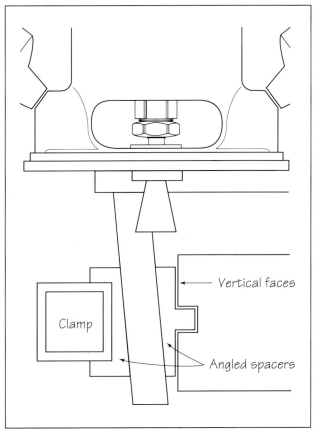

Shop-made spacers are needed to hold pieces in a dovetail jig at an angle for compound miter dovetail joints.

PHOTO 1
Begin the spacers by cutting an angle onto rectilinear stock.

PHOTO 2
Next waste away the area beneath the angle with cuts at the table saw.

PHOTO 3

After a succession of such cuts, the bulk of the waste will be removed. Remove it all for the outside spacer, but leave a central tab for the inner.

PHOTO 4

For the inner spacer, rip off the outside tabs to complete the piece.

PHOTO 5

Spacers, piece and template set to cut dovetails. This photo shows the same configuration as the drawing.

Leigh jig, the inner piece needs a tab to remain to locate it in a slot in the jig base. Leave the central tab as shown in photo 3, then rip off the outer tabs as in photo 4 to complete the part. Photo 5 and the drawing show how the parts are positioned to hold pieces at an angle for dovetailing. Note that if you flip the angled spacers end for end, they will cause the piece to be angled inward, rather than out as shown.

3 CUT THE TAILS, THEN THE PINS

When using any jig for which you cut the tails and pins separately, cut the tails first and then the pins. This is because the adjustment of the fit of the joint takes place on the pin cut, so it should be done after you have tails to test with.

Note that the pin cut must be made with the inside

of the parts toward the jig, whereas the dovetail cut could be made with the inside facing either way. However, because with this jig you set the spacing of the dovetails yourself, the top of each part must face the same direction that the top faced for its mating part. When part A gets its tails cut as in photo 6, its top is to the left. When part B, which mates A, gets its pins cut as in photo 7, its top must also be to the left. What this means is that part A must have its inside facing out when the tails are cut. For this to happen, the part must be tilted outward as in the drawing, but part B must be tilted in, so for the pins, you must flip the angled spacers.

Note that the ends of the parts are cut at 14½° to the top and bottom edges, but the angle of the dovetail tops and pins sides is not at 15°; it is at 0° or perpendicular to the outer edge. Thus the pins come into the tails at an angle to the top and bottom edges, which are horizontal, as in the beginning photo. This makes aligning the top and bottom edges of mating parts somewhat confusing. The solution is to cut test pin pieces until you see how they must be oriented laterally to the template in order to cause the top and bottom edges to line up.

CHAPTER THIRTY-ONE

Colonial Spice Box

WOODS
black walnut

Most of the joinery on this spice box is done with router setups to make sliding dovetails.

SPICE BOX JOINERY

In colonial days, spices were a far more valuable commodity than they are today—and more highly prized—and small glass bottles or metal cans were not as readily available as they are today. So the spice box was made for storing these tasty sundries. Because they were so valuable, hidden compartments were often incorporated into the design of the box to deceive the deceptive.

My modern adaptation of this old box design is joined almost entirely with sliding dovetails, which are simple to set up on the router table. The drawers are made with this joint too, which means that you do almost all the

Hide your—or someone else's—favorite spice in the hidden compartment of this box.

joinery in one series of similar setups. The only other requirements are for other router setups and some table saw work, making this a minimum-tooling project.

1 PREPARE THE STOCK

You'll need more lumber than you might think for this project because of all the drawer parts. There is no sense in using expensive wood for the sides and rears of the drawers, so get a secondary wood for this, like alder or poplar. For the carcass and drawer fronts, choose something pretty, like the figured walnut I used here, as your primary wood. Use your secondary wood for the spacers in between the drawers.

2 GLUE PIECES OF PRIMARY WOOD TO THE SECONDARY WOOD

The next step, after resawing and planing stock to thickness, is to glue thin pieces of your primary wood onto the leading edges of the spacers where they are visible. Clamp up such an edge gluing as in photo 1. When this is out of clamps, rip all your stock to width.

3 CUT THE SLIDING DOVETAILS

Once your stock is prepared to thickness, rip it to width and cut to length. You are now ready to cut the sliding dovetail joints, instructions for which are contained in the next chapter. Cut all the slots to a depth of ¼", and make the tenons the same in length, or just slightly less, but not more. You will be able to do all the tenons on one setup except those on the central vertical spacer, which is thicker than the others (due to the drawer front

Preparing Highly Figured Stock

I chose crotch walnut pieces for the drawer fronts on this box. It's beautiful but must be treated differently than other stock. I couldn't plane it because it would have torn out, and anyway, the parts were too short, having come from a cutoff right next to a huge knot.

You can plane stock such as this with the router planing setup shown in chapter thirty-three, or, as I did here, band saw the parts to thickness (or use a table saw), then belt sand and scrape. Belt sanding with rough grit quickly removes band saw marks, and a scraper quickly removes the Grand Canyons left by the belt sander as in photo 2.

overlap). Do this last. Note also that the tenons on the tops of the sides must fit loosely enough that the top will slide on them so you can get to the hidden compartment.

4 CUT GROOVES IN THE DRAWER PARTS

Set up on the router table with a ¼" straight flute bit to cut grooves in the drawer parts to fit the drawer bottoms. Make these cuts on the sides and backs of the drawers, pushing the pieces along a fence that is set at ¼" from the bit. Use a push stick.

PHOTO 1
Big knots in the drawer spacers are OK so long as the surrounding wood is solid.

PHOTO 2
A sharp scraper quickly takes very rough surfaces to a finish equal to or better than the result of 300-grit sandpaper.

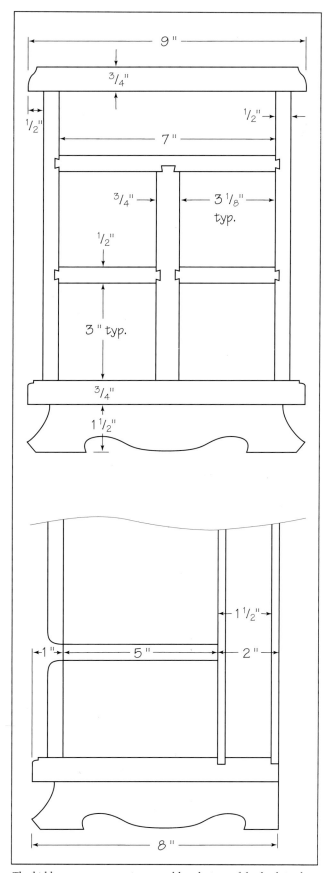

The hidden compartment is created by placing a false back in the box, which is accessed by the sliding top.

CUTTING LIST—COLONIAL SPICE BOX

QUANTITY	DIMENSIONS (IN INCHES)	PART
2	¾ × 8 × 9	top and bottom
1	¾ × 1½ × 30 (approximate)	bottom moulding
1	¾ × 5 × 7	spacer
2	½ × 7 × 9½	sides
1	½ × 5 × 7½	spacer
2	½ × 5 × 3⅝	spacers
1	½ × 2 × 7¾	drawer front
1	½ × 2 × 6⁷/₁₆	drawer back
2	½ × 2 × 5¼	drawer sides
4	½ × 3 × 3⅞	drawer fronts
4	½ × 3 × 2⁹/₁₆	drawer backs
8	½ × 3 × 5¼	drawer sides

Use ¼″ plywood for false and true back as well as drawer bottoms.

Use miscellaneous scrap, cut to fit, for the hidden drawer.

5 CUT THE GROOVE IN THE DRAWER FRONT

The fronts must get different treatment since you don't want the groove to be visible on the ends of these pieces. Use the dovetail slots to help you here. Hold the small drawer fronts in a hand screw as shown in the next chapter, and slip the part over the spinning bit with the bit entering the left-hand dovetail slot. Push forward until the part hits the fence, then push to the left, cutting the groove, until the bit enters the other dovetail slot. Pull the piece away while the bit is in this slot. You may damage a small section of the slot wall, but it will be hidden, and it's not enough to compromise the strength of the whole joint.

6 TRIM DRAWER BACKS

With the slots cut, take all the drawer backs and cut off everything below the top of the groove (½″ or so). These pieces are too short to rip on the table saw safely, so do this on the band saw or by hand. Fit the parts together as in photo 3, and cut bottoms for the drawers out of ¼″-thick plywood. The reason you must cut off the lower sections of the backs is so you can slide the drawer bottoms in over them as shown. Glue up the drawers, slide in the bottoms, and nail them to the back pieces.

PHOTO 3

The drawer bottoms slide into place over the backs, which have been reduced in width. Make the bottoms long enough so they can be nailed to the bottom edge of the backs.

PHOTO 4

The false back fits in grooves in the box sides.

7 CUT SLOTS FOR THE FALSE BACK

While you still have the straight flute bit in the router table, move the fence to 1¾" from the bit, and cut slots on the sides for the false back. This piece of ¼" plywood will fit into the sides as shown in photo 4.

PHOTO 5

The true back fits in rabbets in the sides and bottom. Glue and nail in place.

8 CUT THE RABBETS FOR THE BACK

Next set the fence so it is even with the inside of the bit, and cut a ¼" × ¼" rabbet on the inside rear edges of the sides and bottom but not the top. These are for the true back, which fits onto the carcass as in photo 5.

9 GLUE UP HIDDEN DRAWER

The parts on the hidden drawer are too small to join with sliding dovetails, so just glue them together. I used ⅛"-thick plywood and some ½"-thick scraps, but use whatever you have. Glue the pieces up as in photo 6 (page 112).

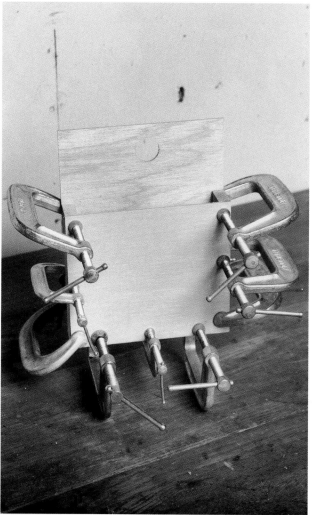

PHOTO 6

Make the hidden compartment out of thin plywood and scrap. To bore the finger hole, sandwich the plywood between two thicker pieces of scrap, and drill through with a spade bit. This prevents tear-out on the plywood.

PHOTO 7

Cut a cove on the edge of moulding for the bottom. See text for safety procedures.

10 PROFILE THE TOP AND BOTTOM

Cut router details into the edges of the top and bottom plates, along the front and sides but not the rear. The box is now ready to be glued up.

11 GLUE UP THE BOX

Clamping this type of joint does not help the glue bond since it cannot bring the mating surfaces of the dovetail tenons and slots any closer. Glue it, slide it together, make sure it's square, and leave it alone to dry.

MAKING THE BASE

The base moulding requires a fairly deep cove cut into it that is larger than most router bits provide. You can

cut a cove like this on the table saw with a setup such as that shown in photo 7. The idea here is to guide the work across the blade at an angle so the resulting cut leaves an arc.

1 SET UP ON THE TABLE SAW

Secure the work on both sides of the blade so it cannot come away from the fence, falling into the blade. Note that the right-hand fence in the photo is a wide piece of 1/2″-thick wood that is held off the table surface with spacers so it is as high as the work being cut. This is necessary because as the cut is made much of the bottom is removed, taking away much of its support. It's OK to raise the blade into this fence so long as its wide enough that it won't get cut in half.

PHOTO 8

Use a band or scroll saw to cut the curved detail on the lower edge of the bottom moulding.

2 BEGIN THE COVE CUTS IN SMALL INCREMENTS

Make the cut *only* in small increments. Start with the blade at $1/16''$ high, pass the pieces over, raise the blade $1/16''$, go again, etc. Use a push stick to keep your hand above the blade. Do not do this procedure with pieces under 18" long.

3 SKETCH THE SHAPE OF THE LOWER CURVES

Sketch the shape of the lower curves on the moulding, and cut it out on a band or scroll saw as in photo 8. Miter the corners of the moulding with the miter gauge at the table saw. Screw a wood support fence to the miter gauge that is long enough to be cut by the blade so the work will be supported directly adjacent to the cut.

WOODSHOP TIP

Smoothing a Rough Curve

When your moulding comes out of the table saw curve cut, it will be very rough. You can sand it smooth by hand, or file the edge of a scraper to the same curve as on the moulding, then sharpen the scraper and use it. You'll save a lot of time.

CHAPTER THIRTY-TWO

Making Sliding Dovetails

USING THE SLIDING DOVETAIL

The only problem with a sliding dovetail joint is that you can't join two pieces with this joint at a corner without one piece or the other overlapping since the dovetail tenon must be surrounded on two sides. So the number of box or furniture designs it can be used on is somewhat limited. Other than that, it's a very easy joint to make at the router table, and you can make many of them quickly.

When you make this joint with very small parts as with the spice box in the previous chapter, you must find a safe way to hold them as they are cut. Sometimes small parts in a router table get grabbed by the bit and thrown, and when this happens, it happens too quickly for you to pull back your hands. If your fingers are close to the bit, they can fall into it after the part is thrown clear. The way to avoid this possibility is to hold onto the part with something else so you can keep your fingers a safe distance away.

DOVETAIL SIZES

Make sure that the maximum diameter of the dovetail bit you use for this procedure is equal to or less than the thickness of the thinnest piece you will put a tenon onto. Always begin the joints by cutting the slots, then make the tenons to fit them. If your parts are small enough to contact a router fence, cut the slots on the router table as in photo 1. If the parts are too long to fit on the router table, clamp a fence to them and cut the slot by holding the router by hand.

MAKING STOPPED SLIDING DOVETAILS

Occasionally you will want to make stopped cuts so the slot does not come out on the leading edge of a board, as with the slots cut on the top and bottom pieces of the spice box. To cut stopped slots, clamp a stop block onto the router table fence as in photo 2. Cut up to the stop, then carefully retract the work.

SLIDING DOVETAILS ON VERY SMALL PIECES

To cut slots on very small pieces, hold them in a hand screw as shown in photo 3. Not only does this let you

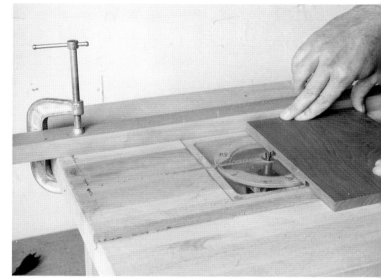

PHOTO 1

The location of the router fence determines the distance of the dovetail slot from the edge of the piece, and the height of the bit determines the depth of the cut.

PHOTO 2

Limit the length of the slot with a stop clamped to the fence.

keep your fingers at a safe distance, but it adds more mass to the body that moves through the cutter. This provides more stability and reduces the likelihood of the bit grabbing the work and throwing it.

CUTTING DOVETAIL TENONS

To cut the dovetail tenons, set up a vertical fence on the router table as shown in photo 4. Make the cut in two passes, one for each side, to put the angled profile on both sides of the tenon.

Adjust the thickness of the tenons to fit the width of the dovetail slots by moving the fence closer or farther from the bit. Note that when you move the fence, the amount you move the fence is doubled in effect on the tenon since you will cut two sides with it. Make test cuts with scrap of the same thickness as your actual parts, and move the fence only slightly when making these adjustments. Ideally you want the tenon to slide in freely with hand pressure only, no hammering. The joints will vary despite your best efforts, so it's best to make them just slightly on the loose side so tight ones will still work.

Note that the final thickness of each tenon depends not only on the position of the fence but also on the thickness of the part itself. It is very important that all your pieces be at the same thickness for similar tenons to result.

PHOTO 3
Safety comes first with small parts. Hold the small part in a hand screw, and use this to guide the part through the cut. Make sure the part is in the clamp such that it is flat on the table and not held up off its surface.

WOODSHOP TIP

Consistent Tenons With Inconsistent Thicknesses

What if your stock varies in thickness? Try this. Set up the vertical fence at a distance that gives the correct tenon with scrap that is close to your average part thickness. Do one side of all your parts with this setup. Next push the fence away from the bit so there is a gap between the bit and fence, a gap approximately equal to the thickness of tenon you need. Now run test pieces through, with the same side against the fence as before. Adjust the fence for a tenon of correct thickness. Run all pieces through with the same face against the fence as they had against it for the first cut; only this time, you are cutting them on the other side.

PHOTO 4
Cut dovetail tenons with a vertical fence at the router table. Use a hand screw here with small parts, too. Don't risk it—use the hand screw.

CHAPTER THIRTY-THREE

Compound Curve Jewelry Box

WOODS
redwood burl

Make a box with spherical sides like this by constructing a special router jig.

WORKING WITH CURVES

Curved work is one of woodworking's major challenges, as well as one of its greatest rewards. Rectilinear designs can have their own beauty, but just as often, they can be rather boring. Any curve, even a single, simple curve, can change the look of a piece dramatically. Use two curves along the same surface, and the piece becomes entirely different in character from other kinds of construction.

But curves have their disadvantages. They are more time consuming to make, and you have to work harder to make parts line up correctly. The more curves you have, the more time consuming it becomes and the more abstractly you must think in order to pull it off.

This project involves the compound, or "complex," curve. In this form the piece is not just curved along one edge, the whole face is curved along two planes. For instance, the front face of the box is curved from right to left on the horizontal plane, and it is curved up and down on the vertical. Because the radii of curvature on both planes are the same, the shape is a section of a sphere.

MAKING COMPOUND CURVES

In the past, compound curves were only made with hand tools. Bombé chests use this idea and are carved by hand, a tedious process requiring patience and skill. Cabriole legs also assume a compound curve and are traditionally shaped with spokeshaves and files.

THE COMPOUND CURVE JIG

You can make this shape using a router and a special jig. The jig itself is relatively easy to build, as is the basic rectangular box that you mount into the jig for shaping. Watching the curved form come out of the rectangle as you operate the jig is a true pleasure to behold. However, before you get to that point, you will need to study the basic geometry involved so you will line everything up correctly.

In this chapter, I will give you two ways to approach the project. Included here are all the details you need for constructing your own jig to your own dimensions if you choose to do so. But if you want a simpler approach, I also give you the exact dimensions I used to make the box shown here so you can simply make that and bypass much of the abstract geometrical conceptualization involved in the process. However, if you do so, you must use a box of exactly the same dimensions and same radii as I used.

That last point may present a problem in some situations. I chose the specific dimensions I did to suit the

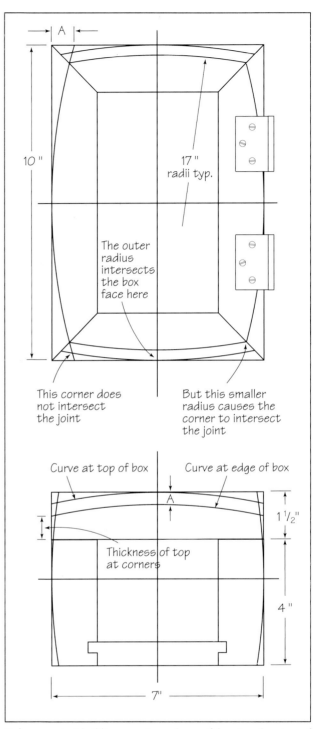

Before you start building your jig, make careful section drawings of the box you intend to make. Test different radii on the drawings to come up with a radius that gives you the greatest curve possible without tapering your parts too much.

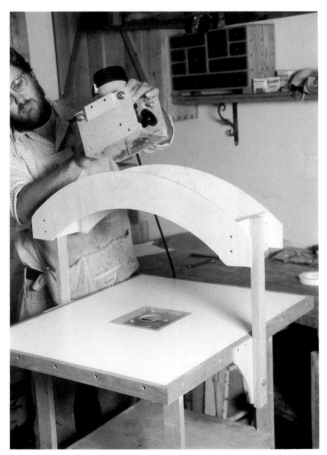

PHOTO 1

The router carriage rides on top of the templates rolling along on four small bearings. Small keepers between the bearings hold the templates against the carriage so the bearings don't roll off.

particular stock I had on hand, a beautiful piece of redwood burl I happily chanced upon long ago. This was the largest box I was able to make with the thickness, width and length of stock I had on hand. If you want to make a box with longer, wider stock, you will probably

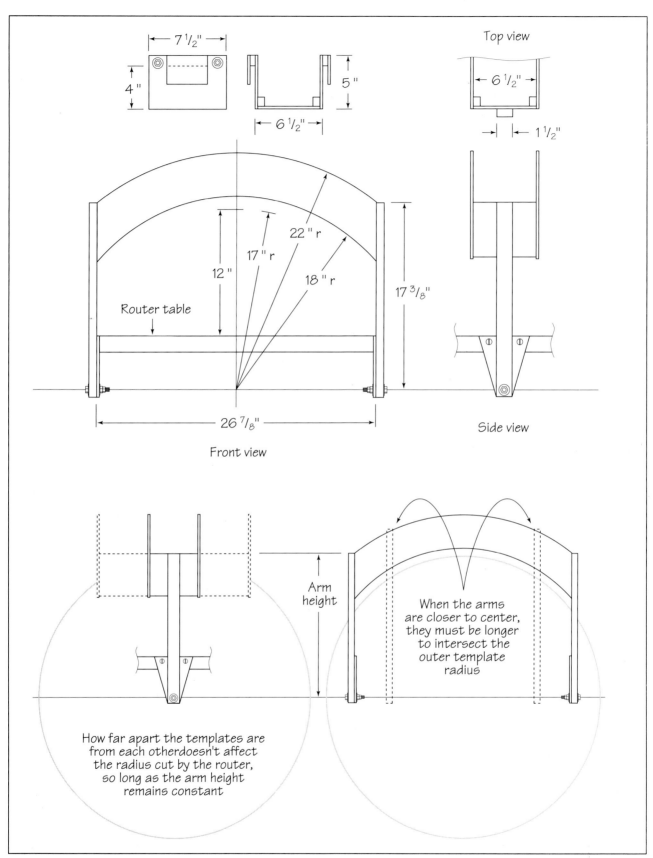

Top view

7 1/2"

4"

5"

6 1/2"

6 1/2"

1 1/2"

22" r

17" r

12"

18" r

17 3/8"

Router table

26 7/8"

Front view

Side view

Arm
height

When the arms
are closer to center,
they must be longer
to intersect the
outer template
radius

How far apart the templates are
from each otherdoesn't affect
the radius cut by the router,
so long as the arm height
remains constant

Make a drawing (full-scale) like that in the lower right showing your radius and how the templates fit outside it. Use this drawing to determine the length of the support arms that hold the templates. Then construct the jig using your own dimensions to suit your box.

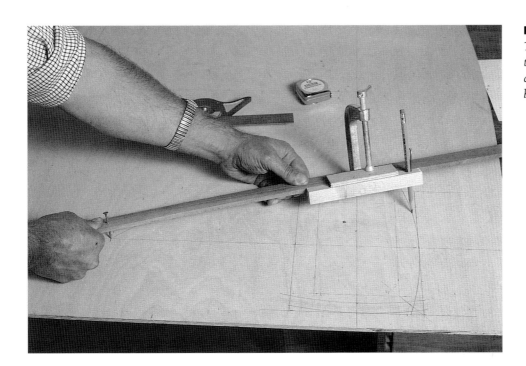

need to use a different radius of curvature, which requires that you redesign the jig.

You could use the dimensions and radii I did for a box that uses smaller pieces of equal thickness, but then you would not be putting as much curve onto the pieces as possible. You may not want to maximize the curve, but be aware that you can use a smaller radius in certain situations, which will give a more rounded box.

WORKING WITH FIGURED WOOD

This project lends itself to using exceptionally figured wood, and since you want to use such wood as efficiently as possible, it makes sense to customize the dimensions and radii to the pieces you have on hand. This becomes even more important when you realize that often you have little choice about what sizes you use when dealing with highly figured wood since the tree decides the size of the burl, not you.

CURVATURE GEOMETRY

When you make a rectangular box, you establish the location of the joint edges before you join them by cutting to length. But with this box, the actual edges will not appear until after the shaping process on the jig. Therefore, you must plan ahead and know where these edges will be so a sloping edge does not taper down to nothing or you cut into the center of the box. To guard against these calamities, make drawings like those on page 117.

Make both of these drawings full scale, and use them to determine what radius is best to use given the dimensions of your stock. For both drawings, first draw a double

center line axis as shown. These axes must extend far enough to locate your radius centers (not shown in these drawings), so make them on a large piece of paper or plywood. Draw in one of the cross sections on each set of axes, one top view and one side view (or front view—either gives you the needed info).

Make trammel points as shown in photo 2 for drawing radii. Now draw in various test radii on the top-view drawing. If your box top is the same thickness as the box sides, the smallest radius you can use will be one that causes the ends of the long box sides to lose about 40 percent of their thickness. Choose a radius that does this approximately, then turn to the side-view drawing and draw in the radius.

But note that on this side-view drawing, you must draw two separate radii on the top. The first intersects the top at its upper surface and represents what the curve looks like in the center of the box. The second curve is lower than the first and represents the location of the curve on the edge of the top. The danger here is that you might choose a radius so small that on the edges it dips below the box corners, effectively cutting away part of the top.

To determine how far below the first radius you must draw the second, refer to the top-section drawing. Dimension A shows you how far down the given radius descends at the edges of a part that is as long as the top. This is true because the front face is as long as the top. Mark out this dimension on the side view as shown, then move your trammel point center that far away from its first location to draw a radius that intersects your drawn line.

The new radius will show you how thick the top will be at the corners, where the thickness is at its minimum. If it is too small to be strong given the wood you are using, you must redraw using a larger radius.

Note on the top-view drawing that there are also two radii shown on the smaller side sections. The first radius intersects the outer surface of the rectangle, but note that if you make the box this way, the corners of the box will not intersect the joints of the pieces. By reducing the thickness of the smaller sides by cutting a second radius, you can make the corners and joints intersect along the curve, which looks very nice and technically accurate.

Another detail not to overlook is the location of your butt hinges as shown in the top-view drawing. Because the back of the box is curved, it is possible to install the hinges behind the curve so the top will bind when opened. To avoid this, install your hinges with the butt centers beyond the farthest outer edge of the back as shown.

MAKING THE RECTANGLE

To join your box parts well with good glue joints at the corner mitres, it is very important that the stock start out flat and straight. However, it is often the case that highly figured woods are twisted this way and that because their fibers are going many different directions, causing excessive distortion during drying. Also, if you face joint and plane figured stock to flatten it, you run the risk of severe tear-out, again because the fibers are multidirectional. If you don't have a jointer or planer, you'll need an alternate means of flattening the stock.

1 PLANE THE STOCK

Use the router planing jig shown in photo 3 for this purpose. Make the jig with a plywood base that has two pieces of wood at ¾″ × 2″ × 24″ screwed to it as shown. These pieces must be straight and their top edges parallel to each other. Then mount your router in a special fixture as shown that rides on the two parallel base pieces. The long rails on the router fixture must also have parallel edges.

Attach your box components to the planing jig base with keeper bars that are screwed to the base. Angle the screws in these bars so that as you tighten them, they pull toward the box component, clamping onto it. Mount a straight flute bit in the router, and adjust the depth of cut to take a minimum off the wood surface, just enough to flatten it. Shim uneven stock underneath so it won't rock during the process. Then flip the part, and plane the other side.

Note that you might not be able to do your drawings as shown on page 118 until after you plane to thickness

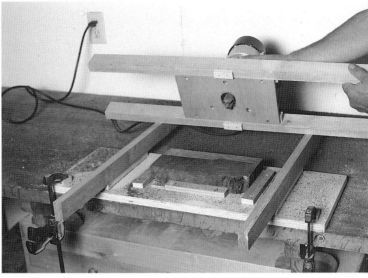

PHOTO 3
When you use this planing setup, be sure you don't set the router bit low enough to hit the screws that hold your workpiece in place.

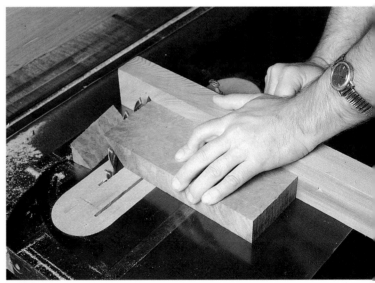

PHOTO 4
Screw a support block to your miter gauge to stabilize the miter cutting operation on the table saw.

because you must first know what thickness your stock will be before making the drawings.

2 CUT MITERS AND GROOVES FOR THE BOTTOM

Once your stock is planed flat, rip it to width, and set up on the table saw to cut 45° miters on the ends of the parts as shown in photo 4. Test your miter setup to be sure that when all four sides are put together, the joints have no gaps. When this is done, put the blade back to 90° and cut grooves for a bottom. Make a bottom with tongues that fit the grooves, and set the alignment of them so the bottom is flush with the sides as shown in the drawing.

3 GLUE UP THE SIDES AND BOTTOM

Glue up the sides with the bottom within them, but don't glue in the bottom so it can move with moisture variations. Use band clamps as shown in photo 5 to apply even pressure to all parts. You can use bar clamps for this, but it's harder to keep the joints aligned as you tighten them.

4 PREPARE THE HINGES

While the box is drying, get your hinges ready. Most butt hinges have the screw holes too close to the butts for this application since you must extend the butts to accommodate the curve as discussed previously. I solved the problem by buying oversized and undrilled hinges, which I then bored for screw holes myself as in photo 6.

5 INSTALL THE HINGES

When the box is dry, install the hinges as shown in photo 7 (page 122). Place the hinges where you want them, and trace their shape with a sharp pencil. Follow the instructions in chapter three for cutting hinge mortises. Finally, install the hinges with your screws. You will shape the box on the router jig with the hinges in place in order to guarantee that the top stays in proper alignment to the sides.

MAKING THE JIG

The purpose of this jig is to move your router bit over the area of a sphere. To do this, you mount your router in a carriage that rolls along the curve of two templates. But this alone would not yield a spherical section; it makes a cylinder. To make a sphere, the templates themselves must pivot.

This seemingly easy task involves careful alignment and preparatory layout to guarantee that the jig will do what you want. The three critical aspects of this are the template radii, the length of the support arms, and the distance between the support arms. Making the templates to a specific radius is easy, but how do you determine the length of the arms that suspend them? It is this length that determines at what radius the templates pivot.

Study the two drawings on page 118 with circles at the bottom. Imagine that the two circles are spheres. The sphere on the right has the jig templates superimposed upon it, along with the support arms. The arms are just long enough so they can contain pivot points that are on

PHOTO 5

When clamping up a box with band clamps as shown, put spacer blocks on the sides of the box to keep the band off the joints. This keeps them free of glue and causes more pressure to be applied to the joints.

PHOTO 6

It's best to clamp down any work you bore on the drill press, particularly metal. Use a countersink to make way for the screwheads.

a line that passes through the sphere center. So long as the arms pivot on that line, they will guide the templates around the sphere in the correct orientation.

Note that if the two support arms were closer to the sphere center as shown with the dotted lines, they would still keep the templates properly aligned. But the arms would have to be longer. The support arms could also be farther from the center, in which case the templates would have to be longer and the arms shorter.

PHOTO 7

Fit the hinges to the box before you shape the box itself. The hinges hold the lid in proper alignment during shaping.

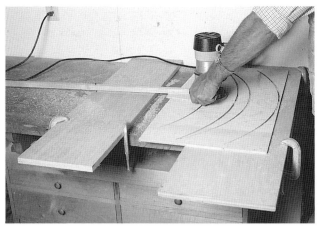

PHOTO 8

When arcing templates with a router, be sure all the plywood is secured to your bench before you make the cut.

The point is that you must determine the proper length of your support arms given how far they are from the center of your sphere and given the radius of your sphere.

Now look at the sphere on the left. This shows the templates and one arm from a side view. Note here that it doesn't matter how far apart the templates are from each other so long as the line from template to template that crosses the top of the support arm stays the same.

The point here is that the exact width of carriage you use, and corresponding distance between templates, doesn't matter so long as you align the templates properly to the support arms.

1 DETERMINE YOUR RADIUS

The first step in building your jig is to make a full-scale drawing of the circle on the right so you can determine how far apart to set your support arms and what their corresponding length must be. Use your trammel points to draw your templates. Note that your templates must be larger in radius than the chosen radius of your box since the router must ride above the box. What is important is that the tip of your router bit be located at the chosen sphere radius. I used a 17" radius, so I made the templates with 18" and 22" radii as shown. My support arm length is set to intersect the 22" radius since that is the top of the templates and an easy reference point.

2 MAKE THE TEMPLATES

Next make the templates themselves with a router arcing jig as shown in photo 8. This jig is just like your trammel points except it has a router on one end. Note that when you locate the jig's pivot nail, you measure from the inside of the bit for outside radii and the outside of the bit for

inside radii. This is to accommodate for the fact that the bit has a diameter, whereas your pencil has a point.

But before you actually cut out the templates, draw three lines on the plywood. The first is a center line, and the other two are for aligning the support arms. Make these two lines equidistant from the center line and at the distance you determined must go between the support arms. When you cut out the templates, be sure the pivot point rests on the center line.

3 ASSEMBLE THE JIG

You're now ready to assemble your jig. The remainder of the drawings in the drawing on page 118 show exactly how I set up mine. My box blank was 5½" × 7" × 10", and by the drawings, I chose 17" for the radius. I came up with 26⅞" for the distance between my support arms by taking 26⅜", the width of my router table, and adding the thickness of two pieces of plywood. Those pieces just provide a spot for the arms to attach to. The width of my carriage was just enough to hold my router base, but you should make your carriage to fit your router. The width between the templates depends upon the carriage.

4 MOUNT THE BOX IN THE JIG

Be sure to give yourself enough room beneath the templates to fit your box along its longest dimension. Mounting the box beneath the templates is the last critical alignment aspect of the job. You must point the center line of the box toward the center of your sphere, then lift the box toward the bit until the two contact at the center line of the box.

Draw center lines on the tabletop of your jig, as well as on the box itself. Make a high 90° holding fixture (I

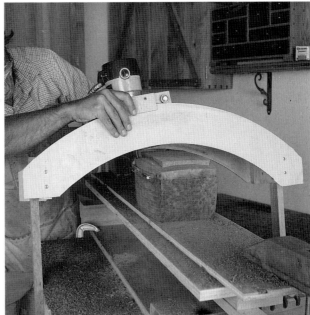

had a tall router table fence handy) to which you can attach the box by means of screws into the box bottom. Draw center lines on this holding fixture, too.

Unplug your router, put in a straight flute bit, set it in the carriage, and set the carriage on the templates as in photo 8. Move it to top dead center. Hold your box and holding fixture beneath, and lift the box until it touches the bit. This shows you how high to locate the box on the holding fixture.

Remove the carriage from the templates, and set it down. Align the box on the fixture at the height you just determined, and line up the vertical center lines. Screw the box to the fixture by screwing into the box bottom. Align the fixture center lines to those on the table, and the box should be in position to shape side 1. Clamp the fixture down so the box will not move while being cut.

5 SHAPE THE BOX

Use masking tape to hold the lid shut while the box is being shaped. Put the carriage back in the templates, and plug in the router. When you switch on the router, be sure the bit is far from any wood. Take light passes at first to get a feel for how it cuts.

Do the back with the hinges after you have done the front and sides so you have a feel for how the router cuts. When you do the back, come no closer to the hinges than ¾″ or so, and take very light passes while in the vicinity of the hinges. Be very careful not to accidentally push the bit into the hinges. After you are through with the shaping process, remove the hinges and carve the wood around the hinge mortises with a sharp chisel to

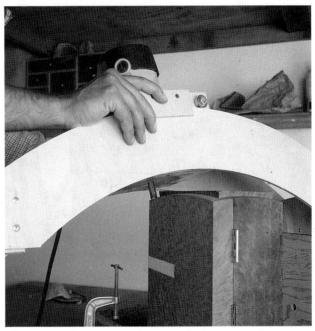

This compound curve router jig causes the jig to move along curves in two planes, which produces a surface that is a section of a sphere.

bring them to shape.

You'll need to make a separate holding device for shaping the box top. Build as many layers of wood or whatever you have to get the box to the correct height on the jig. Be sure you keep track of where your center lines are so you can line them up before you shape, and be sure the box is clamped down solidly.

CHAPTER THIRTY-FOUR

Easy Curved Boxes

CURVES IN ONE PLANE

If the compound curve technique in the last chapter is a bit more complicated than you would like to attempt, here's a method that will give you a box that looks almost as good, with a lot less geometric wizardry. This jig makes a surface that is curved along one plane rather than two, which simplifies the jig a great deal. But before you make a box with this technique, it would still be best to make a drawing similar to the drawing described in the previous chapter because that is the only way you can tell where the final edges of the box will be. You need this information before you begin so you can plan your joinery.

The shape this jig produces is a section of a cylinder, rather than a section of a sphere as in the last chapter. On the box pictured in the drawing, note that while the top is curved from front to rear, it is not curved from side to side. Note that the leading edge of the top is straight, whereas the edges of the top's sides are curved.

DRAWING THE CURVE

This aspect of the design makes your task at the drawing table simpler than with a compound curved box because a cross section of the cylindrical curve, viewed from the side, is the same whether it represents the edge or the middle of the box. On a compound curved box, the edges have lower profiles than the middle, regardless of where it is viewed from. To determine where the edges of the curve will lie with a cylindrical shape, all you need is one cross section drawing with one curve, as shown in the drawing at right.

CURVING THE TOP

A simple way to use this jig effectively is to put a curve into a box top alone as pictured. In this case, you can use a thick piece for the top, as with the compound curve box, but you can use thinner stock on the sides of the box that will not get a curve shape cut into them. Or put the curve into the top and front alone. In this case you will need to make the front thicker than the other sides so there is room for the curved shape. However you proceed, you need to guarantee that the parts you intend to shape are thick enough so that cutting the curve does not interfere with joinery or, worse yet, dive into the inside of the box.

One alternative to consider with a box of this type (or a compound curve box, for that matter) is to join thick box sides with large dovetails before shaping the curve. So long as the sides have a minimum thickness at the internal corner of the joint after the shaping, the dovetails will be strong. Note, however, that this is not necessarily the case with all kinds of joinery. If you use an interlocking joint, as shown in chapter eleven, a tapering face of a box side would ruin the joint if it intersected it. Draw your joint and curve first so you're sure of what you are doing.

SIMPLE CURVE JIG

The jig itself is just a variation on the router planing jig shown in the previous chapter. It differs from that jig only by the curved shape of the outer supports. Make those outer supports with the router radiusing jig shown in the previous chapter. Make them at least a foot longer than the maximum length of curve you plan to shape. This is because the straight support arms that hold the router must hang over the front and rear box edges as they are cut and must be supported in this position.

Make a single center line down the middle of your jig that is aligned with the highest point on the curved support template. Make a center line on your box too, and align it with the one on the jig base as shown. Attach the box to the jig from the bottom with screws. Hold onto the straight support bars as you make the cut, to guarantee that they stay on the curved support templates, and stay close to parallel to the center line.

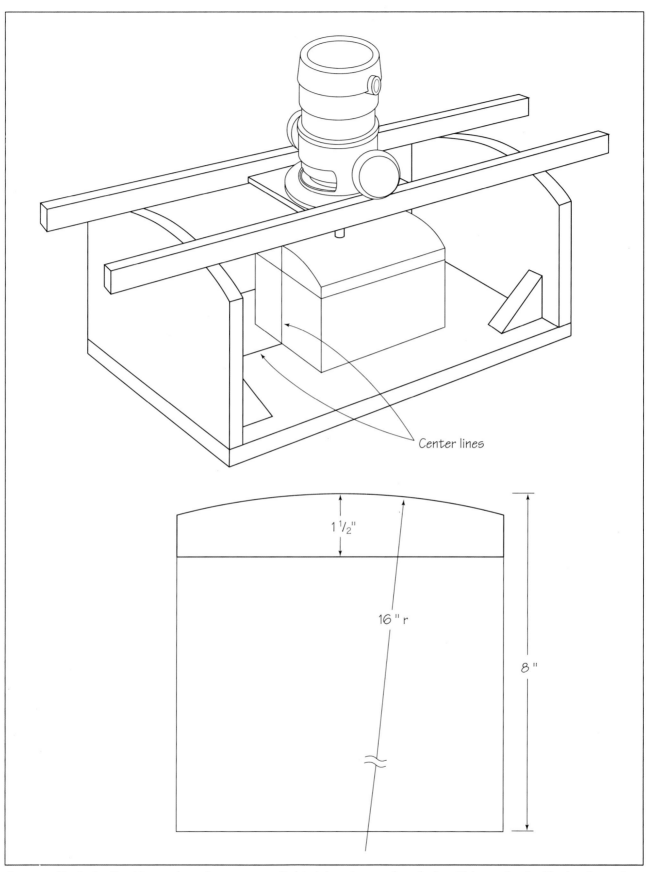

Center lines

$1\frac{1}{2}$"

16 " r

8 "

Construct this planing jig with curved templates to put a cylindrical shape into any face of a box. Make one drawing like that shown above for each curve you plan to cut so you can tell if your chosen radius will work with your part thicknesses and joinery.

CHAPTER THIRTY-FIVE

Sewing Box

WOODS
cherry

This sewing box is light enough to be easily carried to wherever sewing supplies are used.

SPLINED MITERS

My mother once kept her knitting needles and yarn in a cloth bag on the floor so she had to reach down to get what she needed as she knitted. When I saw a sewing box similar to this in an antique shop, the proverbial light bulb lit above my head. (But in keeping with contemporary ecological considerations, it was a compact fluorescent.) It also gave me a chance to try a certain kind of box joinery—a splined miter. This joint is easy to do on the table saw, is quite strong and looks very clean.

1 PREPARE THE STOCK

Begin by getting out your parts and planing down the box pieces to ⁹⁄₁₆″. If you don't have a planer, leave the parts at ¾″; they will look a bit heavier, and you'll need to change a few dimensions here and there, but it will work out fine. Rip the parts to width for the box itself.

2 CUT PARTS TO LENGTH

Cut them to length at the table saw with the blade set at a 45° angle. Make the first 45° cut oversized by ½″ or so, then use the rip fence to set the exact length of the piece for the second cut.

3 CUT GROOVES FOR SPLINES

Leave the blade at 45° to make the groove for the splines as in photo 1. Set the rip fence adjacent to the blade such that the cut is made close to the inside edge of the mitered face, and raise the blade so the depth of cut is ¼″. Make this cut on all eight mitered faces.

4 MAKE THE SPLINES

The grain direction of the splines that go into these joints must be across the joint, not parallel to it, or else the joint could break as the splines split along the grain. For a good glue bond, the splines must fit snugly in the grooves, so their thickness is critical, too.

If you have a planer, you can adjust the thickness of your splines easily. Some planers won't go below ¼″ thickness though. In this case, place your spline stock on top of a larger, thicker piece of wood, and run through the planer piggyback.

If you don't have a planer, make the spline stock on the table saw as in photo 2. Set the rip fence away from the blade at just a hair over the finished thickness you desire, and with a piece of stock about 3″ wide, double rip with the blade height set at half the thickness of the part. Use a push stick to complete the cut. Double ripping this way is much safer than trying to rip the entire face in one pass. You will probably get a bit of burning on the face of the stock from the blade this way, but that can be cleaned up by sanding or hand planing. Bring the stock to a snug fit in the grooves with this cleanup pass.

WOODSHOP TIP

Safety Tip

On the longer sides, use your miter gauge to·support the piece through the cut. The short sides are small enough that the rip fence alone provides enough support for a stable, safe cut.

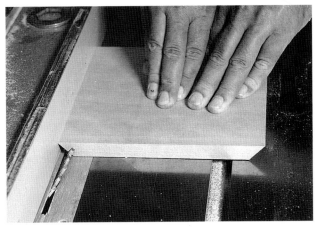

PHOTO 1
Cut grooves for splines on the miter joints with a crosscut or combination blade on the table saw. Make the cut fairly quickly so the blade doesn't burn in the groove. Such burns will inhibit the glue bond.

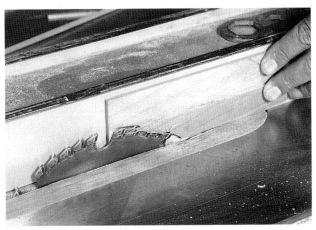

PHOTO 2
Bring spline stock to thickness at the table saw as shown. Use a push stick to complete the cut, and don't run your fingers over the top of the blade.

PHOTO 3
Cut the splines to length with your miter gauge. Regulate the length of the splines with a block clamped to the rip fence ahead of the blade.

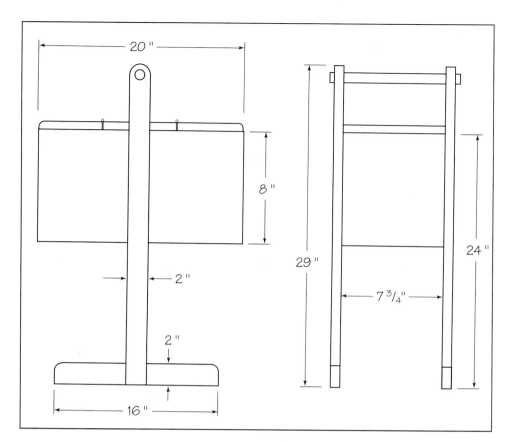

Change the height of the box to suit the needs of the user, but be sure to keep the feet long enough to keep the box from tipping.

Cut the splines to length on the table saw using the miter gauge for support as in photo 3 (page 127). Clamp a stop block onto the rip fence ahead of the blade as shown to set the length of each spline before it is cut. Do not just use the rip fence alone to set this length because if the rip fence lies that close to the blade, the cutoff spline will be trapped between the blade and the fence and will be thrown by the blade. After each spline is cut, use a push stick to clear it away from the blade.

5 CUT DADOES FOR THE BOX BOTTOM

Cut a dado along the bottom of the box sides for the box bottom itself. Make the dado ¼" wide and deep, and set its top edge at a height from the bottom of the sides equal to the thickness of the box bottom itself.

6 MAKE TONGUES FOR THE BOTTOM

Determine the width and length of the box bottom by measuring the inside dimensions of the box and adding onto each of these numbers ½" to account for the tongues. Subtract ¹⁄₁₆" from the width to allow for expansion with moisture variations, and cut out the bottom. Cut the tongues around the perimeter of the bottom with two passes at the table saw. First set the rip fence at ¼" from the outside of the blade, and run all edges of the part

CUTTING LIST—SEWING BOX

QUANTITY	DIMENSIONS (IN INCHES)	PART
2	⁹⁄₁₆ × 8 × 20	sides
2	⁹⁄₁₆ × 8 × 7¾	ends
1	⁹⁄₁₆ × 7½ × 20	top
1	⁹⁄₁₆ × 7 × 18⅜	bottom
2	¾ × 2 × 29	legs
2	¾ × 2 × 14	feet
1	¾ × 10½	rod

face down on the saw. Then set the rip fence ¼" from the inside of the blade. Again run all edges but this time with the part on edge. The resulting tongues will measure ¼" square in cross section.

7 GLUE UP THE BOX

Spread glue in the miter grooves (not the box bottom grooves) with a cheap paint brush. Cut the bristles to about ¾" long. Short, stiff bristles more easily force glue into the narrow groove. Spread glue on the splines, and set them in place. Assemble the box with the bottom in its grooves, and clamp up as in photo 4. Keep the clamps close to the corners or else they will bow in the sides, opening the joints.

8 MAKE THE LEGS AND FEET

While the glue sets up on the box, make the legs and feet. These two join at the bottom with a half lap joint, which is easily made with a dado set and the miter gauge on the table saw as in photo 5. Screw a backup block onto the miter gauge to reduce tear-out on the back of the cut. Regulate the length of the cut on the bottom of the legs with the rip fence as shown. For the feet, make pencil marks 2″ apart and centered on the foot, and cut them out by eye. Make the length of these cuts a bit small to start with, then expand them to fit. The depth of the laps must be half the thickness of the parts so the faces will flush out.

9 INSTALL THE HANDLE

Bore holes in the tops of the legs for the handle rod. Get your handle rod stock before you do this so you will be sure to have a good match between the stock and the hole. Mine came from an old broom handle that happened to be very close to ¾″ diameter and matched the hole made by a Forstner bit of the same diameter. Forstner bits tear out less than other bits and are a good choice here. Set up in the drill press to bore these holes. But if you haven't a drill press or a Forstner bit, you can certainly do with a spade bit in a hand drill. Firmly secure the stock in a vise or to the bench with clamps.

10 FINISH SAND THE LEGS AND FEET

Round over the corners on the feet, as well as the top of the legs. A disk sander with rough grit does this job quickly, but you can also cut out the curves with a band saw or coping saw, and hand sand them smooth.

11 INSTALL THE LEGS AND FEET

Glue the half laps together where the legs and feet join, and secure them with C-clamps. Don't glue the legs onto the box sides because the crossgrain of the box sides will break the glue bond eventually as they expand and contract with moisture variations. Clamp the legs to the box sides, and drill for screws using tapered drill bits with countersinks.

PHOTO 4
Use just enough clamp pressure to close the gaps. More can distort the parts, misaligning the joints.

PHOTO 5
Cut half laps in the legs and feet with a dado set and your miter gauge. If you don't have a dado set, use your regular blade and make multiple cuts. Clean up the rough surface with a chisel.

12 COUNTERSINK SCREWS

Don't install the screws just yet. The same cross-grain forces that work against glue will work against screws unless you make some provision for movement. After you have bored the screw holes, remove the leg from the box and turn it over. Bore countersinks about ¼″ deep on each of the holes (but not far enough to contact the opposite countersink), then replace the leg and screw it to the box. These hidden countersinks give the screw somewhere to go. Plug the screw holes to hide the screws.

PHOTO 6

A shallow rabbet on the underside of the lid pieces gives the top a thinner, more delicate look.

PHOTO 7

Cut hinge mortises in the lid components at the table saw with a dado set or any blade as shown.

13 MAKE THE TOP PIECES

Make the three top pieces from one longer piece so the grain will match. Make the final width and length of these three pieces equal to the width and length of the box itself minus ¼" on both dimensions. Remember, though, that you must cut the piece twice across its width to make the three pieces, so add the width of two saw kerfs onto the length of the top.

Before cutting the top into three pieces, round over the top edges at the router table with a ¼" radius round-over. Then cut a ⅛" × ⅜" rabbet in the bottom of it as in photo 6. Now cut the top into three pieces.

14 MORTISE THE TOP AND INSTALL HINGES

Mortise the edges of the top pieces for hinges with a dado cutter at the table saw as in photo 7. As with the half laps, screw a backup piece to the miter gauge to reduce tear-out at the back of the cut. Also, make the backup piece wide to provide support and to let you keep your fingers well above the cut. The screws you get for small

hinges are usually rather short. Because you are putting these screws into end grain, however, it is a good idea to get longer screws. Screws don't hold as well in end grain; longer ones will give more support. Carefully locate the screw holes so the hinges align the mating parts flush.

15 INSTALL THE TOP

Once the hinges are installed, place the top assembly onto the box, and be sure all fits well. You may need to adjust the rabbets a bit for a good fit. Use small finish nails to secure the central top piece to the box sides.

16 INSTALL THE HANDLE

Slide the handle in place, and secure it with small screws. Install drawer pulls on the doors, and you're ready for the finish of your choice. You can also start thinking of some new garment you would like to wear—like a shirt or a new shop apron—because the proud new owner of the box will probably want to reward you in like kind.

CHAPTER THIRTY-SIX

Making Band Saw Boxes

WOODS

*California bay/laurel
manzanita burl*

Making boxes with the band saw is quick and easy. It allows you to keep the natural form of a rough but beautiful piece of wood, or you can cut graceful curves into a rectangle, as with the box on the left.

PLANNING CUTS

There are a variety of ways to make boxes on the band saw, but they all entail the same basic idea: You hollow out the cavity of the box by cutting out a large central section, then glue back together the outer portions to create the box sides, bottom and top. The trick is to carefully order the succession of cuts so the remaining parts fit back together in the configuration you want. How you cut your wood will depend upon the shape of the chunk you intend to make into a box, as well as whether you want a box with a lid or drawers.

MAKING A BOX OF DRAWERS

Large thick rectangles lend themselves to the drawer configuration, though they could just as easily be oriented horizontally with a long lid if you wish.

You can make shelves for lidded boxes or drawers, if you wish, using the band-sawn technique.

PHOTO 1
Begin a box with drawers by cutting off the back, which will be glued back on after the drawers are cut out.

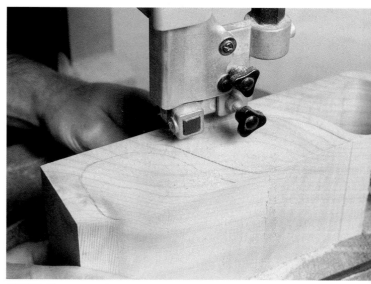

PHOTO 2
Trace the drawers on the front face, rip off a side following the drawer sides, then cut out the drawer blanks.

1 PREPARE THE STOCK

To start a box of drawers, first square up all six sides of the rectangle on your table saw. Note that you need a piece over a foot long to do this safely. Then rip off a thin back as shown in photo 1, at about ⁵⁄₁₆″ thick. Set this piece aside.

2 SKETCH OUT THE DRAWERS

Sketch the shapes of the drawers you desire on the front face of the box. Remember that the radius you can cut on the band saw is limited by the width of the blade you use. Blades are available in ⅛″ width and they will cut very tight radii, but they break easily, so I use ¼″ blades for my tight curve work. Do tests in scrap to see how tight a curve you can cut, and use this as a guide as you sketch your drawers.

3 CUT OUT THE DRAWER BLANKS

At the band saw, rip off one side of the box, following the edges of the drawers you sketched. Then cut out each of the drawer blanks as shown in photo 2.

4 CUT OUT DRAWER FRONTS AND BACKS

The next step is to rip off both the front and back of each drawer blank. Make each of these about ⁵⁄₁₆″ thick or so. As you do this, tilt the piece while it is being cut so the area immediately below the blade is always touching the

band saw table. If you don't do this, the blade could grab the work and throw it down quickly, causing an accident. Keep your fingers out of the path of the blade, and keep your eye on what you are doing.

5 MARK THE STOCK

Mark the front and back pieces of each drawer so you remember where they go. Sketch the inside drawer contour onto the remaining drawer blanks on their front faces, and cut them out as in photo 3.

6 GLUE UP THE BOX AND DRAWERS

Glue up the box carcass and drawer parts as in photo 4. Use a lot of clamps to evenly distribute the pressure. When out of clamps, round over the sharp edges, and sand or scrape the exposed band-sawn surfaces. Finish to your liking, and install pulls that please.

MAKING THE SWIVEL-LIDDED BOX

How you proceed with boxes made of rough pieces such as this will depend upon the shape of the piece you have and what you want to do with it. I'll describe how I made this one, but feel free to alter the procedures to suit your wood and taste.

1 PREPARING THE STOCK

This gnarly burl was crying to be made into a box so it could retain its rough exterior while showing us its figured

PHOTO 3

With the band saw, cut off both the front and back of each drawer, then cut out the cavity of each as shown here.

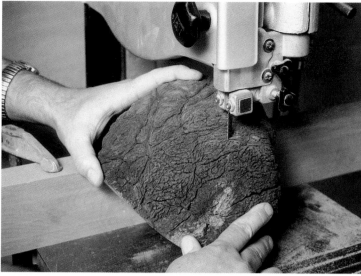

PHOTO 5

On an uneven chunk of wood, first make flat surfaces as I did by making careful cuts on the band saw, referring to a fence.

inside. The first thing I did with it was to cut away the remaining section of attached trunk on the band saw, then I assessed how best to orient the piece as a box. I decided to make the largest flat area into the lid so viewers would see the beautiful burl figure on top.

2 ROUGHING OUT THE TOP

I flattened the broad area that was to be the top with a belt sander and rough grit to eliminate the chain saw marks it had, then I cut off the bottom of the box as in photo 5. By holding the flattened top against a fence as shown, the bottom came out parallel to the top.

3 BORING OUT THE SWIVEL

Next I bored a ½″ hole for the swivel top to pivot upon as in photo 6 (page 134). I carefully set up the drill press so the bit would stop at ¼″ from the drill press tabletop and made the cut from the box bottom as shown. This way the hole didn't come through the box top.

4 CUTTING OFF THE TOP

Then, back at the band saw, I cut off the lid at about ⁹⁄₁₆″ thick. This left about ¼″ or so of the ½″ hole in the underside of the top. Into this I glued a ½″ dowel about 1½″ long for the top to swivel upon. To ensure that the dowel was oriented correctly, I placed it in the box carcass after gluing the other end in the top and checked to see that the lid was parallel to the carcass.

PHOTO 4

Glue the carcass and drawers back together, carefully aligning the parts to each other.

PHOTO 6

For a swivel-lidded top, bore a hole from the bottom toward, but not through, the area that will be the top. Then cut the top off at the band saw, exposing the bottom of the hole into which you can glue a pivot dowel.

PHOTO 7

Now cut out the body of the box. Tilt the band saw table if necessary to accommodate the contours of your wood.

5 SHAPING THE FRONT

To cut out the front portion of the carcass body, I tilted the band saw table to match the angle of the rough surface as in photo 7. But the back portion of the carcass was at right angles to the top and bottom, so I made a separate cut with the table at 90° for that section. This released the central core. From this core I got the box bottom and shelf. The bottom I cut off with a fence to regulate its thickness as in photo 8.

6 MAKING THE SHELF

I made a similar cut to get the blank for the shelf. Then I cut off a thin section from the shelf bottom to make up that part and began to cut out the cavities for the shelf. Once again, I had to make one cut with the band saw table angled as in photo 9 for the shelf front. The other cuts I made with the table at 90° to complete the shelf.

7 MAKING THE BOTTOM

Because of the thickness of the band saw kerf, the bottom fit loosely within its space. But because the front was angled, I was able to drop the bottom down a bit and wedge it in place during the glue-up. When the glue was dry, I flattened the bottom by sanding.

PHOTO 8

This shot shows the central chunk cut out from the body of the box. I'm cutting off the bottom of it to use as the box bottom. Next I'll cut off the top of this chunk to make the shelf.

PHOTO 9

To cut out the body of the shelf, I once again needed to tilt the band saw table to match the angle of the front of the drawer piece.

Adjustable Clamp Company
417 N. Ashland Ave.
Chicago IL 60622
(312) 666-0640
Press screws for making a veneer press, as well as many other woodworking clamps.

AMT Company
P.O. Box 70
Royersford PA 19468
(215) 948-0400
Half-blind dovetail jig, as well as many other woodworking tools.

Bob Morgan Woodworking Supplies
1123 Bardstown Rd.
Louisville KY 40204
(502) 456-2545
Many veneers, lumber, other supplies.

De-Sta-Co
P.O. Box 2800
Troy MI 48007
(313) 589-2008
Wide assortment of toggle clamps.

Craft Supplies
1287 E. 1120 S.
Provo UT 84601
(801) 373-0917
Chucks for turning, other turning supplies.

Eagle America
P.O. Box 1099
Chardon OH 44024
(800) 872-2511
Cope and stick router bits that can be adapted for glazed work.

Hida Tool and Hardware Company
1333 San Pablo Ave.
Berkeley CA 94702
(510) 524-3700
Japanese tools and hardware.

Keller and Company
1327 I St.
Petaluma CA 94952
(707) 763-9336
Dovetail jig.

Klockit
P.O. Box 636
Lake Geneva WI 53147
(800) 556-2548
Clock supplies.

Leichtung Workshops
4944 Commerce Parkway
Cleveland OH 44128
(800) 321-6840
Jointmaster combination dovetail, mortise and tenon, finger joint jig.

Leigh Industries
P.O. Box 357
Port Coquitlam, British Columbia
V3C 4K6
Canada
(604) 464-2700
Dovetail jigs and accessories.

Mercury Vacuum Presses
P.O. Box 2232
Fort Bragg CA 95437
Vacuum press equipment.

Millercraft Inc.
P.O. Box 5586
Derwood MD 20855
Dovemaster dovetail jig.

MLCS
P.O. Box 4053
Rydal PA 19046
(800) 533-9298
Cope and stick router bits that can be adapted for glazed work.

Murray Clock Craft
510 McNicoll Ave.
Willowdale, Ontario M2H 2E1
Canada
(416) 499-4531

Precision Movements
P.O. Box 689
Emmaus PA 18049
(800) 533-2024
Clock supplies.

Porter Cable
P.O. Box 2468
Jackson TN 38302
(901) 668-8600
Omnijig dovetailing fixture, a simpler half-blind dovetail jig, routers and accessories.

Timberline Tool
P.O. Box 673
Medanales NM 87548
Scraper sharpening jig.

Vacuum Pressing Systems, Inc.
553 River Rd.
Brunswick ME 04011
Vacuum press equipment.

Vermont American
P.O. Box 340
Lincolnton NC 28092
Half-blind dovetail jig.

Woodworker's Alliance for Rainforest Protection (WARP)
One Cottage St.
Easthampton MA 01027
Quarterly journal.

Whitechapel Ltd.
P.O. Box 136
Wilson WY 83014
(800) 468-5534
Good assortment of quality cabinet hardware.

Woodcraft
P.O. Box 1686
Parkersburg WV 26102-1686
(800) 225-1153
Scrapers and scraper sharpening tools, some finishing supplies, some hardware, and other woodworking tools.

INDEX

More Great Books for Your Woodshop!

Make Your Own Jigs & Woodshop Furniture—Innovative jigs and fixtures will help you specialize your ordinary power tools without spending big money. You'll get plans for over 40 jigs and fixtures, 23 projects for a well-outfitted workshop and more! #70249/$24.99/144 pages/100 b&w, 100 color illus.

Good Wood Handbook—Your guide to selecting and using the right wood for the job (before you buy). You'll see a wide selection of commercial softwood and hardwoods in full color. #70162/$16.95/128 pages/250+ color illus.

Good Wood Joints—Learn which joints are best for specific situations and how to skillfully make them. You'll discover joints for every application, the basics of joint cutting, and much more! Plus, you'll find an ingenious chart that makes choosing the right joint for the job easy. All well-illustrated with step-by-step instructions for making joinery by machine or hand. #70313/$19.99/128 pages/550 color illus.

Display Cabinets You Can Customize—Go beyond building to designing furniture. You'll receive step-by-step instructions to the base projects—the starting points for a wide variety of pieces, such as display cabinets, tables and cases. Then you'll learn about customizing techniques. You'll see how to adapt a glass front cabinet, put a profile on a cabinet by using molding, get a different look by using stained glass, changing the legs and much more! #70282/$18.99/128 pages/150 b&w illus./paperback

Tables You Can Customize—Learn how to build the tables you want. You'll get furniture plans and guidance in adapting them to your personal needs and skill level. Through illustrations and step-by-step instructions you'll learn how to build four base tables. Then you'll see how to apply variations in joinery, construction, hardware and finishing. #70299/$19.99/128 pages/150 b&w illus./paperback

Blizzard's Book of Woodworking—Step-by-step demonstrations for a wide range of projects for home and garden will hone your skills and improve your technique. #70163/$22.95/208 pages/350+ b&w, 13 color illus.

Pocket Guide to Wood Finishes—This handy guide gives you instant visual guidance for mixing stains and other finishes. Spiral bound and durable— perfect for your woodshop. #70164/$16.95/64 pages/200+ color illus.

Build Your Own Mobile Power Tool Centers—Learn how to "expand" shop space by building mobile workstations that maximize utility, versatility and accessibility of woodshop tools and accessories. #70283/$19.99/144 pages/250 b&w illus./paperback

Creating Your Own Woodshop—Discover dozens of economical ways to fill unused space with the woodshop of your dreams. Self shows you how to convert space, layout the ideal woodshop, or improve your existing shop. #70229/$18.95/128 pages/162 b&w photos/illus./paperback

Building Fine Furniture from Solid Wood—You'll build beautiful wood furniture with 11 of Sadler's most popular projects complete with instructions, exploded drawings, and detailed photographs. #70230/$24.95/160 pages/175 b&w, 35 color illus.

Making Wooden Mechanical Models—Discover plans for 15 handsome and incredibly clever machines with visible wheels, cranks, pistons and other moving parts made of wood. Expertly photographed and complete with materials lists and diagrams, the plans call for a challenging variety of techniques and procedures. #70288/$21.99/144 pages/341 illus./paperback

How To Sharpen Every Blade in Your Woodshop—You know that tools perform best when razor sharp—yet you avoid the dreaded chore. This ingenious guide brings you plans for jigs and devices that make sharpening any blade short and simple! Includes jigs for sharpening boring tools, router bits and more! #70250/$17.99/144 pages/157 b&w illus./paperback

The Woodworker's Sourcebook, 2nd Edition—Shop for woodworking supplies from home! Self has compiled listings for everything from books and videos to plans and associations. Each listing has an address and telephone number and is rated in terms of quality and price. #70281/$19.99/160 pages/50 illus.

Basic Woodturning Techniques—Detailed explanations of fundamental techniques like faceplate and spindle turning will have you turning beautiful pieces in no time. #70211/$14.95/112 pages/119 b&w illus./paperback

Make Your Woodworking Pay for Itself—Find simple hints for selling your work to pay for shop improvements or generate a little extra income! #10323/$16.99/128 pages/30 b&w illus./paperback

Woodworker's Guide to Pricing Your Work—Turn your hobby into profit! You'll find out how other woodworkers set their prices and sell their products. You'll learn how to estimate average materials cost per project, increase your income without sacrificing quality or enjoyment, build repeat and referral business, manage a budget, and much more! #70268/$18.99/160 pages/paperback

The Stanley Book of Woodworking Tools, Techniques and Projects—Become a better woodworker by mastering the fundamentals of choosing the right wood, cutting tight fitting joints, properly using a marking gauge and much more. #70264/$19.95/160 pages/400 color illus./paperback

Woodworker's Guide to Selecting and Milling Wood—Save money on lumber as you preserve the great tradition of felling, milling and drying your own wood. Loads of full-color illustrations will help you identify the right wood for every job. #70248/$22.99/144 pages/128 b&w illus., 32 color photos

Getting the Very Best from Your Scroll Saw—You'll turn to this technique, pattern and project book to learn how to get professional-quality results every time. You'll get directions on it all from cutting dovetails to cutting metal to creating inlays, marquetry and intarsia mosaics. You'll discover how to make puzzles, gifts, games, toys, Victorian fretwork shelves, moldings and much more! #70289/$19.99/160 pages/200 b&w illus./paperback